The Online Educator

RoutledgeFalmer Studies in Distance Education
Series Editors: Desmond Keegan and Alan Tait

The Online Educator

A guide to creating the virtual classroom

Marguerita McVay Lynch

London and New York

First published 2002 by RoutledgeFalmer
11 New Fetter Lane, London EC4P 4EE

Simultaneously published in the USA and Canada
by RoutledgeFalmer
29 West 35th Street, New York, NY 10001

RoutledgeFalmer is an imprint of the Taylor & Francis Group

© 2002 Marguerita McVay Lynch

Typeset in Times New Roman by Keystroke, Jacaranda Lodge, Wolverhampton
Printed and bound in Great Britain by Biddles Ltd, Guildford and King's Lynn

British Library Cataloguing in Publication Data
A catalogue record for this book is available from the British Library

Library of Congress Cataloging in Publication Data
A catalog record for this book has been requested

ISBN 0–415–26369–7 (hbk)
ISBN 0–415–24422–6 (pbk)

February 10, 2004

For Jim,
whose abiding love and support kept me writing
through months of upheaval and change

Contents

List of tables

List of illustrations

List of abbreviations

CD	compact disk
CD-ROM	compact disk read-only memory
CMI	copyright management information
CMS	class management system
DMCA	Digital Millennium Copyright Act (USA)
FAQ	frequently asked question
GIF	CompuServe Graphics Interchange Format
HTML	hypertext markup language
ISDN	integrated service digital network
JPEG	Joint Photographic Experts Group
MOO	MUD, object-oriented
MUD	multiple user discussion/dimension
MUSH	multi-user shared hallucination
KISS	Keep it simple, stupid
PDF	portable document format
Q&A	question and answer
RAM	random access memory
SIS	student information system
TRIP	trade-related intellectual property
URL	universal resource locator
WIPO	World Intellectual Property Organization

Acknowledgments

No book of this scope is written without help. First, I am thankful for the community of distance educators and students who participate on DEOS-L and freely share their issues, concerns, advice, and experience in online education. It is from these postings that I determined what would be important to include in this book. Specific individuals who have been particularly valuable in answering questions, providing Web page resources, and assisting in locating research articles have been Kim Campbell, Mauri Collins, Dennis Roberts, Farhad Saba, Stephen Downes, Julie Whiting, Michael Coghlan, and John Hibbs. I also thank Anna Clarkson and Desmond Keegan for working with me on the book and for allowing me the time to complete it in the midst of a cross-country move. Finally, the book would not be nearly as complete without the undying dedication of my friend and first-reader, Michele Gester.

M.M.L

Introduction

When I was first invited to write this book in late 1999, cutting-edge colleges, universities, and corporate educators were only two years into their initial Web-based distance delivery offerings. At that time I guessed that perhaps 10 percent of colleges and universities in the United States were offering courses on the Web, and perhaps 25 percent of large corporations were doing the same. But statistics for those estimates were very hard to find. I was told that those numbers were significantly lower outside the United States.

Now, in early 2001, statistics about computer use and Web-based training are beginning to surface (though the data are at least eighteen months old). Reports show that close to 80 percent of colleges and universities in the United States are offering Web-based components in their curriculum; 68 percent of K-12 classrooms include some Web-based learning; and over 60 percent of large corporations offer training efforts that use the Web.

The early disappointment of online learning

Unfortunately, anecdotal evidence also suggests that much of this storm of development has been undertaken in haste, without expert preparation or knowledge of the process. In fact, many educational institutions and corporations have approached the development process as a reaction to perceived competition for students, instead of as a project to enhance student learning. The attitude in much of higher education has been: "We need online courses now. I expect there to be x percent of courses by the end of the year. Oh, and by the way, there is little to no extra money to make this happen." The K-12 schools received similar directives, though usually with more political consequences. Politicians want to see schools using technology. Parents want their children competing at the highest levels. Government policies add technology to schools in the same pen stroke that also asks for teachers to be surrogate parents, drug czars, health advisors, and peace officers.

Though this demand for immediate incorporation of Web-based education has yielded a great increase in courses and study opportunities, we are now also seeing the consequences of the absence of strategic planning. This backlash is evident in instructors' refusal to teach online, student protests over receiving insufficient feedback and mentoring from their Web-based professors, parent complaints and fears of children's overexposure to computer-based learning and underexposure to teacher mentoring, and corporate customer complaints that they no longer have access to a "real" person to solve their problems or help them learn. Does this mean Web-based education is doomed? No. However, it does mean that it is time to regroup and look at education from a systems perspective instead of from the perspective that one can slap technology on to an existing system and make it work.

Embrace change and become an active participant in it

Change is a constant companion of education and the larger governmental and even global system in which education functions. We have become a global learning society. As such, our educational systems must become a primary vehicle for assisting learners to become successful citizens of the world – a world that demands new knowledge, new thoughts, new frameworks for problem-solving, and new ways of caring for one another. Education must change much of what it does and how it does it in order to become a contributing partner to our new realities. With the advent of this global communication network, called the Internet, education finally has the ability to go beyond the issues of local reality and mold global reality by shaping citizens through education. Sound a bit idealistic? Perhaps. But, the reality is that the Web is changing the world – changing businesses, changing the way research is shared between countries, changing the way government communicates both locally and globally, and changing the way individuals communicate. Education has always been an integral part of shaping individuals. Now those individuals may exist all around the world at any one moment in time.

Change – inevitable as it is – continues to be perceived by most educators as a threat. The question for educators is whether to be a part of the change or a victim of change. Too often, as educators, we have allowed others to make system-wide decisions for us. Too often, we have behaved like bystanders, reacting to change rather than being proactive planners or active participants and contributors. The communication capabilities of the Internet provide us with the opportunity to help create the kind of educational environment we want for tomorrow's students. An action-oriented approach requires systematic and formal planning, design, implementation, and evaluation to take place. Most of all, we need to develop a new vision of education for the Internet age.

In this new global communication technological environment, we must also embrace other disciplines and use their best practices to develop an action plan to enhance teaching and learning. In the past, education and training have not fared well in most organizations. In higher education they have been held closely within the purview of college and university "education" departments that have been charged with training teachers in the K-12 environment. In addition, university educators generally receive no education or teaching training at all. Rather, they are valued for their specific research expertise without regard to their ability to teach. Corporate education traditionally relegates employee training to the human resources department to fight for budgetary prominence along with the importance of recruiting new employees. Customer training education is consigned to the marketing department – that realm of illusion and half-truths. Is it any wonder, then, that an attempt to suddenly bring education and technology to the forefront of an organization may run into trouble?

Web-based education, unlike the traditional classroom, requires the marriage of many different views in order to be successful. Certainly, its foundation lies in well researched educational principles. However, with this global communication network, technology becomes of equal importance in order for education to be effective. In addition, because computer and video interfaces embrace a graphic-oriented presentation approach, one must also marry art, technology, and a little marketing to the presentation of education. No longer can we depend on the speech-making artistry of the lecturer to imbue students with knowledge. Now education must work closely with departments that were traditionally not a part of the study or delivery of education. Also, now the student becomes an active participant in the education process and the instructor must take on a mentorship role rather than the sage role.

The three foundational rules of Web-based education

The first rule in Web-based education is that we must push beyond our comfort zone. We must venture beyond the known, acceptable, and conventional. Our current frames of reference, boundaries, and assumptions must be challenged at every turn. We must undertake fundamental change in the way we think about educational partners. If we stick to only what is comfortable, we will likely fail. We will quickly find ourselves reaching outmoded or incomplete conclusions. Once we have embraced the concept of "out of the box" thinking, we will be well on our way to step two.

The second rule in Web-based education is plan, plan, plan, and then do more planning. Both the beauty and the beast of the Web is in its static information nature. It is beautiful in that information can be cataloged, indexed, and cross-referenced for use in many courses. For those who love to work with mind maps and dream of providing simulated cognitive pathways to learning material, this myriad of possible paths to information is a welcome system in education. However, the beast of the Web is that too much information quickly becomes overwhelming. It is easy to lose track of where the information can be found. Frequently, links are changed, outdated, moved, or dropped without notice – leaving you and your students without some important piece of data. The only way to work within this environment is through extensive planning. Plan for contingencies. Plan for support structures. Plan for fluidity of thought within a loose framework of the course. Above all, plan for constant change by providing a framework to deal with problems.

The third rule in Web-based education is that interactive communication is paramount. Many texts have quoted the phrase "interaction, interaction, inter-action." One cannot emphasize this enough. Unfortunately, too many developers have taken it to mean provide a quiz every third screen or force students to log in every day and count the number of logins in their grade. Neither of these is a good example of interaction. Effective interaction requires communication – not regurgitation and not repetition. Interactive communication comes in the form of demonstrating *thinking* processes. Some interactive forms include reflection papers, active discussions with the instructor and with class peers, taking leadership roles in presenting what has been learned, mentoring, coaching, problem-solving, and a myriad of forms of analysis, synthesis, and evaluation. Think of the "interaction rule" espoused in many texts as always linked with communication. If students are not actively communicating their learning process to teachers and peers then they are not interacting.

How to use this book

A book of this scope does not lend itself to a linear path that would lead you step by step through the process of building an online course or creating an entire Web-based environment. In systems development many things happen simultaneously and many steps require returning to previous steps. Thus the format of this book is more like a Web-based course.

Each chapter contains information around a specific category. You may wish to approach the text from beginning to end, following the imposed format of one approach to design or you may choose to delve into those chapters that address your particular problem at the time.

The imposed format in many ways begins in the middle and then returns to the beginning. It begins by assuming a reality where Web-based education already exists in some form and thus begins with a problem: "What is wrong with online education?" In answering this question, the book then provides potential solutions to the problem by returning to the systems development cycle beginning with the students' needs, addressing support systems and faculty, and then zeroing in on individual course development decisions and assessment of the course and the students. The final chapter is a potpourri of information that is not easily categorized but certainly addresses important issues and current difficulties in online education. The chapter finishes with a discussion of current trends and predictions for the future of online education.

Finally to assist you with the myriad of Web sites and resources listed in this book, I have provided a Web page with all the links activated. You may access that page at http://web.pdx.edu/~mmlynch/Routledge-book/routledgebookweb.html.

I hope you find the book useful. Even more, I hope you add to this collection of experience by sharing your problem-solving ideas and best practices with others so that all of us in the global education community may benefit and become active participants in building global citizens.

1   Planning for online course/ curriculum delivery

No matter which instructional design model you favor, each one emphasizes planning. Whether on the system level or on the course element level, planning is a step in the design process that cannot be overlooked. When beginning to plan for an Internet course, in addition to all the usual problems of planning a class that must fit within a curriculum and an entire course of study, one must also plan for the added factor of the Web-based delivery environment.

We are still in an age where teachers, parents, and students are asking if all the hype around Web-based learning has any basis in fact. Do Web-based courses really improve learning? And what kind of investment and effort does it really take to build and maintain an effective learning community within each course and within the institution as a whole? According to the National Education Association in the United States and numerous research articles published in the past two years, the answer is a resounding "Yes" for the effectiveness of Web-based learning. The investment of funds and effort can be returned tenfold over the course of a year. However, you are forewarned that it will take considerable funds and effort to start up and to plan a maintenance schedule. If you can survive the pain of that first year or two, then you are well on your way to providing a thriving Web-based learning environment.

The positive aspects of this environment have been hyped in marketing brochures, in the popular press, and by a variety of software and hardware sales people. Certainly, many of these are accurate: instant access to information, the ability to involve students and instructors from a variety of locations, helping students to become familiar with the computer-based environment that permeates business, and enhanced communication across a wider learning community. Additional benefits that have been documented in research include:

- *All course content is in one accessible location for students and teachers.* Resources, materials, handouts, homework assignments, and grade tracking can be available twenty-four hours a day, seven days a week. This cuts down on requests for information.
- *Different learning styles can be addressed.* Graphics, audio, video, and other media reinforce instruction, while communication functions such as e-mail and threaded discussions enable timid students to express and develop their thoughts.

- *Active learning is increased.* Because Web-based courses increase efficiency, there is more time for active learning and application of concepts. Electronic communication technology also provides new possibilities for interaction outside of the formal classroom environment of lectures and note-taking (e.g. role-playing, discussing case studies).
- *Learning communities are fostered.* Web-based courses build a new kind of community that is not bound by location or time. No longer are students relegated to meeting and talking with only those who can stay after class or meet for lunch.
- *Students enjoy using a variety of media to learn concepts and theory.* Today's students are technologically savvy and accustomed to using the Web.

Certainly, the ability to capitalize effectively on each of these positives is important. Techniques for enhancing them will be discussed in later chapters.

Of course, not every facet of Web-based education paints such a rosy picture. Less discussion has been documented about the known problems with Web-based education and how to address them when planning your online courses. Specifically, this chapter will address problems with:

- Access.
- Retention.
- Isolation.
- Learning style adaptation.
- Enhancing the student's ability to generalize knowledge to the new environment.
- Motivation.
- Time management.
- Academic integrity.

Access

Almost three decades ago, Nelson (1973) envisioned a global system of interlinked information sources that would provide access to all the world's information resources for all the world's citizens. In 1973, this may have been viewed as idealistic futurism at its best or implausible science fiction at its worst. It is only since the explosive growth of the Internet that Nelson's theoretical construct has begun to enter the realm of practical implementation and use. However, today we are still a long way from realizing Nelson's dream. Today, three key factors continue to hamper this increased access: technological infrastructure, investment resources, and language and cultural differences.

Those who are studying distance learning and those whose career involves the use of computers often make the mistake of believing that "everyone" has access to the online environment. Unfortunately, this is far from the truth. Preliminary 2000 census figures in the United States show the percentage of computer users at approximately 68 percent. Of course the number of "users" does not necessarily mean the number of individuals who have access to the Internet at home, which is estimated at approximately 34 percent.

Technological infrastructure differences

In other countries the percentage of computer users at home is far less. In fact, in many European countries the mention of the word "online" immediately creates images of expense and unaffordability. Unlike the United States, it is still a common practice for most Internet providers to charge by the minute for access, and those charges are limiting to many people. Furthermore, in nations such as Indonesia, Brazil, Russia, or Angola, where the telecommunication infrastructure is not as developed or as freely accessible as in the United States, Europe, Australia, or Singapore, significant funding and personnel resources still need to be provided. Table 1.1 summarizes estimates of the number of users in a variety of countries around the world. For many nations, the use is so small that statistics are not even available.

In spite of all these difficulties, Internet use is growing and will continue to grow. The *Computer Industry Almanac* predicts that worldwide Internet users will be near 6.73 million at the end of 2002, and will exceed 1 billion by the end of 2005, with the majority of growth coming from Asia, Latin America and Eastern Europe. Table 1.1 lists the top fifteen countries in Internet users at year-end 2000 and the percent of those countries' total population Internet users represent.

Furthermore, even in the resource-rich United States, surveys such as that of those homes that do have a computer show that its primary use is for entertainment. It is an inescapable fact that the majority of Americans have no previous experience or knowledge of using computers for learning.

In addition to the larger infrastructure within countries or communities, a personal computer level of infrastructure can severely impact access. This personal

Table 1.1 Top fifteen countries in Internet users at year-end 2000 (million)

Country	Weekly users	All users	User % of total population
USA	114.4	134.6	47
Japan	25.4	33.9	27
Germany	14.9	19.9	24
Canada	13.1	15.4	51
UK	12.6	16.8	28
South Korea	12.4	19.0	40
China	11.3	22.5	2
Italy	9.3	12.5	22
France	6.3	9.0	15
Australia	5.3	7.6	40
Taiwan	4.5	7.0	32
Netherlands	4.1	5.5	34
Sweden	3.8	5.6	49
Spain	3.6	7.5	14
Russia	3.0	7.5	5

level of access is expressed through the students' selection of connectivity and browsers.

- *Connectivity speed* creates a challenge for Web-based course developers. Will the student be accessing courses through a dial-up connection (speeds of 28.8 kbs or 56 kbs), through a cable modem, a DSL or ISDN line, or through a satellite dish? The speed of access is a significant determiner in the designer's selection of media. Those with a 56 k connection will not welcome the use of video clips, audio clips, or many graphics. Those with a faster connection will be bored with text-only applications.
- *Connectivity providers* also create problems with access. Students accessing a course through a large commercial provider, like AOL, have different issues from students accessing through a small local provider or from those accessing through their work or university provider. Many help desk support personnel have pulled their hair out attempting to troubleshoot the large variety of connectivity issues.
- *Servers and browsers* are the final and possibly most problematic connectivity issue. Server software resides on one computer and allows individuals to access Web pages that also reside on that computer. Browser software is the "decoder" used to view those Web pages.

   Usually, neither students nor developers have much control over the server. It is provided by some central resource on campus or through a commercial provider. It may be UNIX, Linux, Windows NT, MacHTTP, or any number of other platforms. The key question for the designer is: "What aspects of the server may I use? Can I access the server for database queries, storage, interactive forms, etc.?"

   On the browser side, the last few years have narrowed the list to two browsers used by approximately 97 percent of Internet users – Netscape Communicator and Microsoft Internet Explorer. The other 3 percent of users fall into specialty browsers like AOL's integrated browser or browsers favored by some developers and programmers (e.g. Lynx, Opera, Powermarks). The difficulty with the selection of browsers is that Web pages display slightly differently on each browser. The designer must at least ensure the pages are effective on the two top browsers.

   Note: For free browser statistics software to check your users, try SMS-FF Corporation's Web site counter and statistics generator at: http://www.globalserve.net/~smsff/perl/browsers/index.htm.

Need for investment

So how much difficulty is involved in providing access even in technologically developed nations? For rural areas of the United States, as well as most of Europe and other technologically developed countries, the current infrastructure cannot cope with the traffic that has resulted from the exponential growth and use of the Internet, both in terms of information providers and in terms of end users. Many nations are currently attempting to cope with the signs of overextension, particularly at certain times of the day. There is still significant need for continued investment of funds and personnel even for richer nations. In some countries this infrastructure is beginning to be provided by private business partners. In others the national government is footing the bill. Yet there are still many countries that simply do not have the resources for this type of investment.

Language and cultural differences

Language is a critical issue in determining how courses will be offered in a world-wide market. Should your courses be in the local language of the originating course developer? (In many countries the "local" language already encompasses two or three required languages). Or should all courses designated as "worldwide" in your curriculum be agreed to follow a common language? If so, which language should be selected?

Even when a common language is selected, you must also be alert to the fact that there are substantial cross-cultural differences in interaction and communication beyond the actual words being used on the Web. Furthermore, culture goes far deeper than that associated with a specific country or region. Any organization develops its own norms and expectations of communication. For example, a Web-based environment that emphasizes student-centered learning and student choice in navigation may not be consistent with a hierarchically oriented culture. Many education models around the world have a culture of the teacher as "god" and the student as a vessel to be filled. Other cultures, like that of the United States, are beginning to change to a consumer-based educational model, where student choice is paramount.

Beyond the basics of language selection and cultural educational models lie differences in content and purpose shaped by politics and culture. How does the designer of a worldwide course begin to determine content for a cross-cultural course?

Collis *et al.* (1996) discussed several guidelines based on the european experience in the "TeleScopia Project," which focused on adapting courses for trans-European delivery. Four of those guidelines relate directly to this issue.

- *Language.* Be cognizant of differences in communication styles, such as who should moderate discussions, who should initiate questions, how much debate is allowed or expected, and who should be allowed to end the discussion. The expected formality must be explicit within the course.
- *Interaction.* A requirement for heavy interaction among participants may be seen as a burden by some cultures. In a cross-cultural context, the designer must make a decision as to whether all students will be expected to participate at the same level of interaction or will it be variable depending on the countries or cultures involved in the course.
- *Content.* Either select content where cross-cultural aspects are minimal (i.e. computer programming courses that have an expectation of a specialized skill

that is already accepted worldwide) or develop lessons and assignments where cross-cultural aspects are an integral part of the content (i.e. international business issues or cross-cultural ethics).

- *Visualization*. Consider the use of graphics and charts to represent concepts instead of text. Text and word choice leave much open to misunderstanding and misinterpretation. Visualizations that replace or supplement text have a better chance of being accepted and understood.

Internet access and Web publishing policies

Access and publishing policies usually fall into two categories: (1) policies around the funding, use, and security of the Web server; and (2) policies around the creation, publishing, and security of specific Web pages. The degree to which your policies must be detailed is in direct relationship to the scope of your Internet capabilities and the access you want students and teachers to enjoy and use.

Server access

Internet access is an expensive and complex undertaking. As a result, it is wise to have in place a policy that specifies who can access the Internet and under what circumstances, what can be accessed, and who pays for the service. Organizational policies on providing Internet service to students and teachers range from providing free access via the organization's local area network to requiring students and/or teachers to access the organization's Web pages via a commercial provider. Institutional policies may include reimbursement of all or some of the user's cost to access the Web pages. Factors to consider in an internet access policy:

- Do you want to provide access to students?
- Do you want to charge a fee for that access (added to tuition, a technology fee, a per-minute fee, etc.)?
- What type of access are you willing to support (remote dial-up, on-campus network only, an 800 number, twenty-four hours a day/seven days a week)? How often will students be required to connect?
- What communication protocols are you willing to support (e-mail, chat, threaded discussions, whiteboard)?
- What type of reliability can you guarantee students and instructors?
- Can you separate your Web-based classroom server from your administrative server?
- How much disk space will be allocated per department? Per course? Per instructor? Per student?
- Will courses/pages be password-protected?
- Do you want to use a secure server for other student information associated with courses (e.g. student identification, grades, financial aid, etc.)?
- What alternatives, if any, exist for students without access?

Web page publishing policies

Many organizations have begun to specify policies around what types of Web pages are allowed on their server. These policies may stipulate format, content, usage, or even specific software to use in creating the Web page. Some institutions (particularly in the K-12 arena) even have inspectors who must scrutinize and recommend every page before it is allowed on the server. Such policies are usually designed to control consistency and quality. Whatever level of control your organization desires, it is important that the policy be clear and explicit in its detail. Factors to consider in a Web page publishing policy are:

- Do you have a format you wish to promulgate for all Web-based courses? A common template provides a consistent image of the institution and assists students in consistent navigational structures from one course to the next.
- Is there an approval process for content, quality, and/or structure? If so, who is the person or group that must approve all pages?
- What type of support structure are you willing to provide to teachers and students who need to place Web pages on your server (e.g. technology skill-building courses, help desk support)?
- In what format is the content material currently? Do you want it to be converted to a usable Web format or to start development from scratch?

Retention

There are two issues surrounding retention in the Web-based learning environment. First, do students retain what they learn on the Web as well or better than in the classroom environment? Second, what about statistics concerning high numbers of students who drop-out of Web-based classes? Each of these will be addressed separately.

Do students retain what they learn on the Web?

The dawn of the Internet has provided a significant increase in the availability of information. However, to date there is little research about weather the availability of information translates to an increase in learning and retention. Do students learn differently in the online environment? How is information used differently from a face-to-face classroom?

Yanni (2000) provides some insight into student learning by observing how students do research in the technology-rich library environments available today. From the standpoint of research skills, he found that students are learning *different* skills – technology skills – to a greater degree, and faster. For example, students learned to retrieve adequate information more quickly. They also mastered techniques of storage and retrieval of information, and how databases are organized.

Even more impressive is Neill's (1998) finding that students gained more subject knowledge through research in a shorter period of time, allowing them more time to organize the information in their minds, think, and allow learning to take place – metacognition. In this example, students not only learned more, but they also learned *how* to learn.

Unfortunately, the news is not all good. There is also a group of students who quickly access information without evaluating or caring about the source and then placing the information in their papers or homework. The learning process ends soon after the homework assignment is completed and no retention occurs. These students use the Internet and quick access as a means to accomplish an objective (complete their homework or get a degree) without the goal of actual learning.

How does an instructor ensure that students meet Neill's criteria of effective Web-based research rather than simply accessing information without undergoing the learning process? The key is to allow time for processing and to provide assignments that encourage and check metacognitive functions throughout the assignments. Mere access to information is passive. It is up to the instructor to make learning active. For example, Campbell (1998) suggests that writing and reflection are key elements for processing and internalizing information.

Providing activities that require analysis, evaluation, and application will also require more mental processing and enhance learning and retention. How to provide these activities in a Web-based environment will be discussed in detail in future chapters.

What about the drop-out rates of Web-based students?

Several articles were written between 1995 and 1998 about high drop-out rates in Web-based education. Many educational institutions (both public and private, as well as corporate training centers) measure their success by student retention numbers. These numbers look to evaluate the retention of students throughout the class, the retention of students throughout a curriculum, and the numbers of students graduating with certificates, diplomas, or degrees. Thus retention of students in the online environment is very important.

By 1997 the majority of US colleges and universities were reporting averages ranging from 30 percent to 75 percent of students not completing Web-based courses. Consequently, a great deal of research began around the issues of student retention. As might be expected, the answer was not a single issue. Some of the issues most frequently quoted include:

- *Technology.* Students expressed frustration concerning access to technical support. Many students reported spending as much time trying to resolve technical problems as they did learning the content of the course.
- *Experience.* Since most students have little experience of learning at a distance, they are unfamiliar with it and may be anxious about taking distance education courses. This unfamiliarity is translated into resistance. Also, students did not know how to communicate effectively with their instructors, and thus they expressed discomfort at not having the instructor's input to guide them.
- *Lack of teacher feedback.* Two related difficulties provide a great deal of

frustration for students – timely instructor response and vague instructor-to-student communication.

> . . . students' concerns about receiving prompt, unambiguous feedback continued throughout the term . . . many of the students worked on the course during the late evenings and weekends . . . What is needed is for the students and instructors to learn how to manage their expectations about when they should be able to have reliable, fast communicative responses.
>
> (Hara and Kling, 2000)

- *Online miscommunication*. Miscommunication by the teacher or student, or both, can obscure learning expectations. Specifically, students want tools to help them monitor their progress. Also, teacher mediation during courses needs to be increased.

So what is the answer to the dilemma of high student drop-out? First and foremost, both students and faculty must receive a good orientation to the online learning environment. This should include not only learning about the technology of the environment, but also learning about how to use the environment effectively for communication and enhanced learning. McVay (2000) found that by requiring a student orientation course drop-out rates decreased by more than half. In courses averaging student drop-outs ranging from 35–50 percent the rate was reduced to 8–15 percent.

In addition to an effective orientation course, there are a variety of support structures and processes that may decrease frustration and assist students' transition to Web-based learning. Certainly, implementing them will help to enhance retention.

- Consistent access to the Internet
- Tutoring services
- Consistent methodologies for completing and submitting assignments
- Protocol for student–instructor communication
- Online access to library or research services
- Registration and tracking
- Online bookstore access

Isolation

It is interesting to note that distance education and isolation have gone hand in hand for more than forty years. In the beginning, isolation was mentioned as a painful struggle for distance students who could not make it to the classroom location. Later, isolation was named as the culprit in miscommunication difficulties between students and teachers. Then, as Web-based education emerged in the late 1990s, isolation was again cited as a potential problem, with traditional instructors arguing that students were missing so much of the social context of the classroom. On the other hand, researchers have been applauding Web-based education as a means to "break the isolation of typical classrooms . . ." (Donlan, 1998), allowing students to experience people, places, and activities not available in other ways and to make learning more enjoyable and engaging.

Isolation can be a problem in Web-based learning and it can affect student success in the online environment. However, isolation occurs because of poor course design – not as an inherent result of a Web-based delivery system. In fact, several studies now point to students feeling more connected with their instructor and peers in the online environment than they do in the classroom environment. The key is for the designer to make the Web-based course as rich or richer in interpersonal interaction than a classroom-based course, knowing that the language of physical presence is absent in the online environment.

Course design

Following the logic that effective course design is the primary component of online student success, Harasim (1997) concluded that most course design does not exploit the tools of the Internet to present information and increase interactivity. Specifically, she suggested that course design must include the following to be successful.

- High rates of student participation
- Group interaction among students
- High quality of intellectual exchange
- Spatial metaphors used as mental models to help students adjust to an online structured course

Physical isolation in Web-based learning is a given. Students are accessing information from a location other than the classroom. However, physical isolation does not need to transfer into mental, social, or emotional isolation. A major problem that designers must address is the lack of information given to students about the course, the student performance expectations, and the lack of experience many students have with learning online. Some of this can be addressed in an orientation course, as previously suggested. However, the manner in which the instructor conducts the course and his or her availability to the student will make the biggest difference on a course-by-course basis.

To overcome the feeling of isolation created by the loss of a physical classroom, instructors need to provide various methods of interaction with the students.

- *Electronic office hours.* Most teachers have some type of office hour arrangements for their traditional students. This same arrangement needs to be made for Web-based students. Select certain times when you will be available via chat or e-mail for immediate responses. For example, a college professor who would normally have three hours per week might select electronic office hours as in Table 1.2. Frequently, instructors will select a variety of office hour times

Table 1.2 "Electronic office" hours

Week day	Communication method	Availability GMT
Tuesday	Discussion board	9.00–10.00 a.m.
Wednesday	E-mail	7.00–8.00 p.m.
Sunday	Chat	1.00–2.00 p.m.

in order to meet the varied needs of students in different time zones or with different work/family schedules.

- *Setting the mood for "safe" communication.* As students cannot see body language or easily judge personality when an online class begins, it is important for the teacher to model acceptable communication and to encourage student contact early in the course. This can be accomplished by use of the following methods.
  - *Send a welcome letter,* via e-mail, to all students enrolled in the course. Include praise for undertaking the course, encouragement for their success, your expectations for their participation, and how to contact you throughout the course.
  - *Model a communication style* with your first postings to the class discussion board (formal or informal). If you want discussions to be formal, well written, using outside references, then make your first posting in that format and explicitly detail your expectations to the students. If you prefer a free flow of ideas and discussion without attention to the details of formal writing, then open the discussion with a question or concept that is written informally and encourage students to do the same.
  - *Invite students to introduce themselves* to you and to each other, adding information that may be ancillary to the specific course (e.g. hobbies, outside interests, how the course fits into their personal/professional goals, etc.). Again, model the introduction process by posting an introduction of yourself.
  - *Share your own real-life experiences* as they relate to the discussions and encourage students to do the same. Providing relevant, real-life experiences allows the students to make direct connections between theory and practice.
  - *Check-in with students regularly* by making contact via e-mail and/or the discussion board. Some instructors send a weekly e-mail to all students that summarizes the class's progress, provides notes of encouragement, and reminds students of upcoming projects. Others use a weekly announcement Web page or an announcement section of the discussion board for this purpose. Simply responding to students' posting on the discussion board with comments, criticism, or encouragement will show that you are connected with the students and care about their progress.
  - *Encourage mentoring among students* by having them lead discussions, suggesting partnership assignments, and matching different perspectives on a problem as part of their learning process.

Through good course design, active participation by both students and the instructor, and encouragement toward self-disclosure and reflection, designers can turn the potential problems associated with isolation into the positive of opening up the isolation of the classroom to an entire world of interesting ideas, people, and activities.

Learning style adaptation

For many years educators have noticed that some students prefer certain methods of learning over others. These learning styles form a student's unique learning preference and, left to the student's natural tendencies, can enhance or hinder his or her ability to grasp a concept and apply it in the future. There is also much controversy among educators as to whether learning style preferences should be considered in designing instruction and whether a style not addressed negatively affects student success. There seems to be research supporting both sides of this issue with a plethora of variables to consider. The best approach is probably to be aware that learning styles exist and to determine what impact, if any, that knowledge should have on your course design process.

The nature of the Web tends to be graphical and textual, thus catering particularly to those with a *visual* learning preference. Those with auditory or kinesthetic learning preferences frequently find themselves at a great disadvantage in the Web-based learning environment. This is particularly true of the hundreds of courses that exist today containing only lecture notes and little interaction or mentoring.

Kolb's (1986) popular learning style inventory, which is often used in distance learning research, measured student preferences in two bipolar dimensions. Kolb suggested that over time learners develop either a preference for concrete experiences or a preference for engaging in abstract analyses when acquiring skills and knowledge. Students may also emphasize interest in turning theory into practice by active experimentation, or they may prefer to think about their experiences by reflective observation. Dille and Mezack (1991) used Kolb's inventory to identify student success in Web-based learning. They found that students who preferred abstract analyses did much better than those with higher scores in concrete experience. Terrell and Dringus (1999–2000) found that Kolb's converger and assimilator categories were predictive of greater success in their graduate degree program.

Given these findings, do they mean that visual, abstract learners should be the only ones advised to undertake online studies? Or is it up to teachers to develop online learning strategies that somehow meet all different types of learning preferences? The answer lies in a shared responsibility for learning between the instructor and the student. The teacher needs to vary the online teaching strategies to include a variety of styles (e.g. graphics, text, opportunities for kinesthetic application, interaction with peers and instructor, and reflective time). This helps provide a style that not only caters to individual learners, but also reinforces concepts using a variety of methods that will likely help all learners.

More important, the students need to become aware of their preferred learning style and how to adapt it to the Web-based environment. When students were made aware of their learning style in an orientation course, McVay (2000) found that students improved their ability to learn and improved their success rate in completing future courses by nearly 94 percent. Furthermore, they demonstrated the ability to discern their preferred learning styles and adjust them as needed to accommodate differences in the distance environment from one class experience to the next. Catering to a variety of learning styles is as important online as in the classroom; but offering students the means to shape their own learning is the most powerful tool an instructor can provide.

Generalization of mental models

An important part of student learning is described within the conceptual framework of the students' ability to generalize their mental models to the new environment. Jonassen (1995) suggested that learners will generalize existing models to new phenomena through a process known as structure mapping – linking the old structural relations to new ones. However, frequently within the online environment students have not been given analogies to use for this structure mapping process. Carly and Palmquist (1992) examined this further by elaborating five specific characteristics of successful mental models.

- Mental models are internal representations.
- Language is the key to understanding mental models.
- Mental models can be represented as networks of concepts.
- The meanings of the concepts are embedded in their relation to other concepts.
- The social meaning of concepts is derived from the intersection of different individuals' mental models.

These characteristics all presuppose a language and relationship between concepts that allow students to derive meaning. It would then follow that if students are not provided with instruction or assistance in formulating the relationships and interactions, they may not be successful in generating the necessary new mental models.

In addition to increasing the "human element" in the student-to-teacher interaction, as described above, it is also important to provide students with customized tools to support instructional activities, learning activities, and the design and integration of multimedia. These tools begin with a good student orientation that allows students to practice skills in the new online environment and begin to draw analogies and relationships with their experience of classroom-based learning. Then, on a course-by-course basis, it is important for the designer to continue to provide similar analogies that relate the new content back to the relationships experienced in the orientation course. Table 1.3 provides examples of classroom-based activities and the analogous experience possible in the Web-based environment. Each encounter the designer plans to use in future courses should be experienced in the orientation course first. This provides a safe environment for students (and faculty) to practice the skills and build their mental models prior to having to use the experiences under the stress of grading and excellent performance.

Table 1.3 Translation of classroom-based interactions to the Web

Classroom interaction	Form of Web interaction	Description of potential use
Class discussions	Chat room: synchronous, immediate interactivity	Schedule specific chat times when students may gather to discuss a topic. It is useful to structure the chat by providing questions or topics in advance.
	Discussion board (bulletin board): asynchronous, gives time for considered responses	Post questions on the discussion board and ask for student responses. Ask students to share learning reflections on the discussion board and/or to post assignment progress.
Role-playing	Discussion board (asynchronous)	Students are assigned a role and a scenario that will be played out asynchronously on the discussion board. Students log in within specified time frames (e.g. one week) and respond within their defined role parameters to solve a problem or create further analysis and discussion.
	MOOs/MUDs Chat (synchronous)	Students come to the role-play in assigned roles; a scenario can be previously posted on a Web page. Students then interact in real time within their role parameters.
	Virtual world (synchronous)	Students interact in real time in a graphic world (like a computer game) where they are either assigned a role or create their own role to play within the environment. Frequently the world will also allow them to create their own physical representation (avatar) to move about the virtual world.
Case studies	Chat (synchronous)	Provide a case study in advance (via textbook or Web pages) and ask students to come prepared to analyze the case during chat.
	Discussion board (asynchronous)	Post specific case-related questions to the discussion board. Students post a response to instructor questions. They also post disagreements, critiques, or agreement with other students' thoughts.
	E-mail (asynchronous)	Ask for a written analytical assignment to be attached to e-mail and sent to the instructor for review.
	Virtual world (synchronous)	Students participate in a graphical world (like a computer game) where they interact as a character within the case and solve problems.
Question-and-answer sessions	Discussion board (asynchronous)	Designate a topic on the discussion board for Q&A to be used throughout the class. Or create a

		series of subtopics with frequently asked questions and answers that lie under the major topic of FAQs. Or have students create or update FAQs.
	Chat (synchronous)	Hold chat office hours posted in advance as described in a previous section. Have student study groups form and meet in chat to prepare for tests or assignments. They may work from a prepared set of questions or generate their own.
Assignments and peer critiques	E-mail attachment (asynchronous)	Students send attachments to the instructor via e-mail for grading and feedback. Students may also send papers to other students for electronic editing, comments, and feedback.
	Web page (asynchronous)	Students post work to the Web and send the URL to the instructor and/or other students for review and critique/grading.
	Discussion board (asynchronous)	The instructor or student copies portions of assignments (using cut and paste functions) for sharing with the entire class.

Source: Table expanded from its first publication in the Technology Source (McVay, 1998). Used by permission.

In addition to the above translations, it is possible that the Web-based learning environment would include facilities for telephone conferencing (audiobridge) and/or video conferencing. This may be done over the Internet using Web-based audio and video software, or using other facilities to supplement the Internet delivery (e.g. CD). The full implementation of the technologies in the matrix and the audio and video technologies are discussed in greater detail later in the book.

Motivation

Motivation in online learning has become an issue that is related primarily to the experience of high drop-out rates in Web-based classes. However, distance educators have long been concerned about motivation in other distance delivery formats as well. Holloway and Ohler (1991) spoke to the issues of learner motivation by suggesting that distance learning technology design or use does not make the performance of learning tasks rewarding. Other researchers, however, clarified these issues of motivation by specifying five factors that are indicative of student success in distance education.

- Intention to complete the course
- Early submission of work
- Completion of previous distance education courses
- Degree of interaction provided in the course
- . Course relevance to the student's real-world experiences

Certainly, some of these factors can be addressed through course design. However, some of them can be addressed only through the personal intervention of the instructor or an advisor. Both solutions should be employed simultaneously to ensure students remain motivated throughout their online learning experience.

Course design

Several researchers suggest that a situated cognition model is necessary to ensure learning success. Providing application of theory is a mainstay of good instruction whether online or in the classroom. Keller and Burkman (1993) agree with the situated cognition model and specifically present numerous guidelines for the design of motivational courses. They define the guidelines in terms of four categories: interest, relevance, expectancy, and satisfaction. The key guidelines as they relate to Web-based instruction in these categories are below.

Interest

- Vary the content organization and presentation.
- Use active voice and action verbs.
- Provide opportunities early for students to interact with the instructor, each other and the content.
- Provoke debate by introducing contradictory opinions.
- Appeal to different learning styles.
- Challenge students to compete among themselves.

Relevance

- Show how instruction relates to the learner.
- Be an instructor who is also learning new things.
- Build a strong relationship between the objectives and the outcomes.
- Teach in a problem-based manner that applies knowledge to real-world situations.

Expectancy

- Make the course navigation appear easy.
- Organize the instructional text for easy access and write in a readable style.
- Follow good graphic and text design principles.
- Be explicit in the expectations of student participation and quality of assignments.

Satisfaction

- Provide opportunities for students to use the new skills and knowledge in the real world.

- Frequently reinforce learners as to their standing in the course and what they can do to improve and/or maintain high course values.
- Reward accomplishment with positive feedback.
- Share excellent work with others – student peers and other institutions.

Interpersonal intervention

There will always be students who are high achievers and immediately turn in work, participate well in discussions, and take an active role in learning. This is true in traditional classrooms as well as Web-based classrooms. Likewise there will always be students who seem to struggle to manage their time, turn in assignments late or not at all, and either don't show up for discussions or stay in the background letting others speak for them. The difficulty in Web-based instruction is identifying whether a student actually fits into the latter category or has "fallen through the cracks" of technology and doesn't know how to contact you. Without explicit guidelines, help desk support, or instructor intervention it is possible – even probable – that a good student will be lost early in the course and simply drop out owing to frustration with the system.

Cornell and Martin (1997) articulated a number of possible interpersonal interventions that are available to instructors who are dealing with seemingly unmotivated students in the Web-based environment. Five key points are listed below.

- Get to know the students. Ask for introductions and submission of individual biographies.
- Ask for photographs, phone numbers, and e-mail addresses.
- Communicate with students early and regularly. If some students are not participating, contact them by phone. Perhaps there is a computer glitch.
- Avoid confrontation, sarcasm, or putdowns. Assume the students want to succeed, and ask how you can help make that happen. An honest expression of concern for students' well-being will often turn the situation around.
- Provide early and continuous feedback of students' academic standing and offer suggestions for improvement.

The bottom line is to be actively involved in the facilitation of the course and of student learning. An active instructor facilitating a well designed online course will have significantly fewer problems with student motivation. In fact, research has shown that an active instructor will encourage active students and the students then report high levels of satisfaction with the online learning model.

Time management

A frequent complaint from online instructors and course designers is the amount of time it takes to develop and then facilitate a Web-based course. The issue of development is one that is true of any quality curriculum development, traditional or online. The amount of time it takes to develop a course is reflective of the adherence to good learning principles and teaching strategies. Certainly a Web-based course takes some additional time, as there is a learning curve for using the technology and then the implementation of multimedia aspects of a course. However, with technology permeating the classroom environment, some of this is also inherent in any course design today. Specifics of course design are discussed in further detail in later chapters. Here we will focus on the time management aspects of teaching or facilitating a Web-based course.

The first problem that arises in Web-based courses is the inundation of student need for contact. Many instructors report that they seem to be always answering e-mail and thus have little time for other interaction with students and little time for providing quality feedback on homework assignments. Then, past the e-mail dilemma, are complaints about the time it takes to *read* all the discussion forums in which students participate.

It is certainly true that the Web-based environment creates significantly more reading requirements for both teachers and students. It is also true that the immediacy of Web communication sets expectations of instant response that many facilitators initially try to meet. They then tire quickly of Web-based learning environments and the toll it takes of their time. The only way to alleviate this situation is to have an effective time management plan, to clearly articulate your plan to your students, and then to faithfully adhere to the plan. There are five basic tenets you need to include in your time management plan.

- Plan specific activities for the time you would have normally allocated for classroom attendance in the course.
- Plan specific days and times that you will be available for office hours.
- Set aside specific days and times allocated for evaluating student homework, discussion board participation, chat transcripts, etc.
- At the beginning of the course, make it clear to students what your availability plan is so they have clear expectations of your feedback and turn-around time.
- Key your homework turn-around time to specific due dates (if it is a time-dependent course) instead of to the date the homework is received by you.

The key is to schedule specific times, let your students know what those times are, and then stick to your plan. For example, in a four credit hour college course in the United States you would normally be expected to be present in the classroom (lecturing or facilitating learning activities) for four hours per week. In addition to that time, it is likely that you have some requirement for office hours for that class – say two hours per week. Finally, there would also be a requirement for you to evaluate students through their participation and homework.

In the online environment, you plan to spend that four hours per week of "classroom" time in answering student e-mail and reading student discussion board and chat transcripts. As an example, you might schedule from 9.00 a.m. to 11.00 a.m. on Tuesday and Thursday for those activities. It is important, therefore, to let your students know that these are your days for answering e-mail for this particular class so they don't have an expectation of immediate answers when they've sent their message at midnight on Sunday. This would then constitute the four hours per week you would normally schedule for the class. In addition, you would select two hours per week for chat office hours. It is advisable that you select times that are most likely to match with the majority of your students. If your students are working adults who normally log on to the course at night and on the weekends, then it is important for you to select corresponding office hour times. Finally, determine and articulate what your turnaround time will be on homework assignments. For example, you may state that all homework feedback will be returned within one week of the final due date for the assignment. Again, if you don't specify your turnaround time, students will expect feedback within twenty-four hours. This can create havoc when you have some students handing in assignments two weeks before they are due and others waiting until the last moment, depending on their individual learning schedules.

It is important to design a time management plan that lets you maintain your sanity and meets the needs of your students. Though many teachers may initially feel the desire to answer e-mail every day and turn around homework within forty-eight hours, they would soon find themselves overwhelmed – particularly if they have more than one course to teach online. There is something to be said for setting an example that life is not always one of immediate satisfaction, nor is it reasonable to expect that just because the Internet allows us to communicate twenty-four hours a day, seven days a week that we must do so. It is best to establish good habits and set student expectations early on. In that way, as you take on more online courses you will not find yourself among those instructors who beg to return to the classroom simply because they've overloaded their time.

Academic integrity

The issue of academic integrity, like many of the issues discussed in this chapter, comes from two perspectives. (1) How comparable are learning standards between online and more traditional classroom formats? (2) How do we deal with student cheating in the online environment? Both of these issues are ones that have received a great deal of press in the past year, as well as some actual research. The issue of academic rigor arouses suspicion that Web-based students can receive better grades for equivalent learning or equivalent grades for learning at a lower level of mastery. The issue of academic integrity refers to the confidence that work leading to recognized achievement is the student's own work. Both of these issues are also important to the traditional learning environment, but, because of technology, they take on a special concern to anyone who is trying to determine whether a Web-based delivery method is viable for their organization.

Academic rigor – comparable standards

The rapid expansion of online education opportunities throughout the world has raised many concerns among academics. A persistent question is how comparable are learning standards between online and traditional formats. At stake is the confidence that educators will have in the validity of academic credits earned online. Some of this concern stems from alarm at the increasing number of diploma mills that have become a part of Internet offerings. Other concerns stem from a question about the role of the instructor in facilitating learning in the online environment, as well as the integrity of online courses.

The key to ensuring academic rigor is to develop courses to meet the same goals and objectives as their classroom-based counterparts. Most institutions that have been providing traditional courses do not change their course goals and objectives, nor do they change the means by which to assess student mastery of those goals and objectives. In this way, one can easily make comparisons between similar courses and the delivery method. Ridley and Husband (1998) compared grades of students in online classes versus traditional classes and found that actually students in the traditional classes had a slightly higher grade point average (0.3 higher on a four-point scale) than students in the online classes. Perhaps we should ask ourselves if, in our attempt to ensure academic rigor, we have made the online classes more rigorous and thus at a disadvantage.

If you are developing a Web-based class that has no traditional counterpart, the key still lies in following good instructional design principles. Define the course goals and objectives, create instructional strategies for delivering the material and encouraging active learning, and link the objectives and strategies with the assessment you will use to determine mastery. If you consistently apply those principles, academic rigor will be ensured.

Deterring cheating

Given the ease of copying and pasting plagiarized material and the alarming number of Web sites that offer term papers for sale, it is not surprising that cheating has become a major problem in many educational institutions. Some statistics put the rise of cheating at 20 percent of the student population. The issue of academic cheating online usually falls into two categories. (1) How do we know the person at that remote computer is the person registered for the class? (2) How do we know the student hasn't plagiarized his or her paper, discussion board response, or e-mail response?

Identity crisis

Solving the identity problem is not an easy or inexpensive proposition for an institution. On the technological side there are a variety of security-based programs that can be installed, ranging from simple password assignment to something as complex as fingerprint identification and eventually retinal scans. For those who don't wish to invest in this technology, there is always the option of having proctored settings for key exams or papers. This involves setting up approved proctors and/or proctor sites where the student's identity is checked and the student is observed during the exam or the writing of a paper.

Both of these options leave much to be desired. From a course design perspective, it is better to create course activities and assessments that will make it more difficult for students to cheat through demanding a specific frequency of participation as well as a type of participation that requires student application of theory to their own lives. To pay someone else to participate quickly becomes very costly.

Plagiarism

There are now a number of Web-based search engines that can compare a student's work – by looking for matching words – with electronic library resources, Internet research papers that have been posted by their authors, as well as those for sale on disreputable Web sites. Depending on the search engine, you may get a report of what words in the student paper match exactly to known resources. If plagiarism is of great concern to your organization, you may wish to download a free trial copy to try it out. Some of the more popular search engines are listed below with their current Web site addresses.

- Eve by CaNexus at http://www.canexus.com/eve/index.shtml
- IntegriGuard at http://www.integriguard.com/
- Turniton at http://www.turniton.com
- Glatt at http://www.plagiarism.com/screening.htm
- Word Check at http://www.wordchecksystems.com/

However, even if you decide to purchase one of these search engines, it is unlikely that you will have the time or desire to feed every student paper and correspondence through the engine. These are reserved more as a check of your suspicions about a particular student. Just as in a traditional classroom, the online teacher begins to form a knowledge of his or her students' manner in expressing themselves, both formally and informally. It is only when something is submitted that doesn't match the student's style that you would elect to use the plagiarism search engine.

Furthermore, the same methods of course design that help to deter identity cheating also help to prevent plagiarism in the online environment. Your first steps should be to develop a plan of student awareness and an organizational code of honor. Here are a few tips for deterring plagiarism in your online classes.

- Make sure students understand that when they copy something from the Web it is the same as copying something from a book. Believe it or not, many students do not know this.
- Have students sign a contract of understanding and agreement not to plagiarize. This may not stop them, but it will make them think twice.
- Strictly enforce the rules when you discover plagiarism (e.g. a failing grade on that paper, dismissal from the school, etc.).
- In your student orientation course to online learning include a module on plagiarism. Have students work through examples where they are required to

identify whether the example is plagiarized and, if so, how the reference should have been cited.
- Provide an online class environment that requires a great deal of interaction in both formal and informal discussions, writing papers, and working with peers.
- Include at least one telephone discussion or a time when the instructor phones the students for a "check-up chat." Ask how the student is feeling about the class, question the student about recent difficult concepts and offer assistance for learning those concepts better.
- If you use a final exam or competency exam that must be proctored, then work to pre-approve acceptable proctors and sites well in advance (e.g. local college faculty, teaching and learning center personnel, librarians, military personnel, church pastors, etc.).
- Focus on field-based application of concepts. For example, when teaching a business communications course online, require students to give a presentation in a business environment and to have it critiqued by a manager. The critique form is then forwarded to the instructor. You need not grade them on the critique scores themselves, as you cannot control grading curves from one manager to another. However, you may elect to grade students' reflection papers describing their experience in giving the presentation, what they learned from the critique, and how they will improve in the future.

The goal is to make it unlikely that a "cheater" could pay someone enough to consistently go to this length to participate for them in a course. Furthermore, because the assignment information is not static, it is unlikely the student will easily find a paper to purchase that meets the requirements of the assignments.

Even more important, each of these suggestions is simply good course design practice. Not only do they help deter cheating, but they also provide a better learning environment for students. Any time you can make the course material more relevant to their real-world experience they will retain more of the concepts and be able to apply them in future.

2 Assessing student needs and subsequent system requirements

The purpose of all instruction is to enable students to learn. In order to do that effectively, you must begin by understanding your students' characteristics, their specific needs in the Web-based environment, and how you might plan to meet those needs. In a perfect world, the design of online instruction would be so flexible that it could adapt to each student's needs as he or she progressed through the course. However, we do not live or work in a perfect world and to date neither the technology nor the time is available to build such a perfect system. Student characteristics are widely different and frequently competing. The designer must then decide what needs can be addressed and how best to address them within limited budgets and time frames.

To begin the process of needs analysis, it helps to ask some important questions about your specific student population.

*   How old are your students?
*   What cultural and language backgrounds do they have?
*   What prior educational experience do they have?
*   Are they pursuing an individual course, a group of courses, or an entire degree program?
*   What disabilities or challenges might they have in the online environment (i.e. hearing or sight impaired, unable to use a keyboard)?
*   What technology skills do the students have?
*   What written communication skills do the students have?
*   How open are the students to a shared leadership or ownership model of learning?
*   How open are the students to change?

Once you have answered these questions you will be able to build a profile of student characteristics to serve as the foundation for building your online environment and your individual courses.

Typical student population characteristics

There is a great deal of research into the characteristics of students who select distance education – interactive television, correspondence courses, and videotaped instruction. More specific research has begun to emerge about those who choose Web-based learning. Not surprisingly, the characteristics of "distance" students and Web-based students turn out to be very similar. Below are summaries of four student populations studied in the online distance environment: elementary students, secondary students, at-risk students, and adult learners (which encompasses both college students and workshop training through businesses).

Elementary (grammar school) students

Though the Web is frequently used in elementary schools today, the public school system rarely uses it as the only form of education for this group of students. The conventional wisdom still strongly believes that most students, age 5–12, need to be in a traditional classroom environment. This required classroom environment is favored not necessarily because the content is best delivered this way, but because it is agreed that the face-to-face environment is more supportive of the social development of the child. Given this stricture, the Web serves primarily as a means to deliver content and to provide some unique capabilities for interaction with the content via Web-based activities. The Web also provides access to other people and potential shared curriculum around the world. The traditional classroom then serves as the host for social, cultural, and general maturation activities that are best done with children within a face-to-face setting.

The Web-based teaching format for entire courses in the elementary school environment has risen most quickly with those students categorized as "home-schooled." The home-schooled child is defined as one who is receiving his or her education entirely at home – or at least physically separate from any school building (public or private). Home schooling occurs for a variety of reasons.

- Family-specific religious or political beliefs find home schooling more effective for instilling particular moral, political, and ethical values.
- Student physical or learning disabilities have been determined to be best met within a home-school environment or an environment that provides direct one-to-one attention.
- An accelerated student who is bored in a typical classroom needs the additional challenges provided in a home-school environment.
- The family home location is far removed from transportation services to get the child to a traditional school (i.e. farm, ranch, or tribal community).
- Frequent family relocation makes the consistency of home schooling better suited to the child's education than attempting to fit into a large number of school environments in a single year.

For home-schooled children, the use of Web-based learning has provided a wealth of resources and information that previously was not readily accessible. The ability to find courses in a variety of important topics has also provided better consistency of learning. For example, the parents of one child may feel very comfortable teaching math and science subjects because it relates to their work environment but may feel less sure of their ability to effectively teach history and social science. The Web provides a host of prepared courses available to those parents, as well as a network of other home-schooling parents and organizations that willingly share ideas and curriculum. As these loosely affiliated organizations of parents become more familiar with the Web-based environment, it is feasible for them to form parent partnerships and share resources. In the future, it may not be uncommon for parents to barter trades in teaching roles (i.e. parent No. 1 will teach math online to six children around the country while parent No. 2 teaches history to those same children, and parent No. 3 teaches writing skills).

Several examples of home-school resources and partnerships associated with Web-based learning are currently found in university education centers, in school districts, and in parental organizations. Below are a few examples of the type of Web support available to home schools.

- Central Valley Home School http://www.centralvalleyhomeschool.com/
- University of Missouri http://cdis.missouri.edu/homeschool.htm
- Nebraska Christian Home Educators' Association http://www.nchea.org/
- Jon's Home School Resource Page http://www.midnightbeach.com/hs/

In addition to home-school options, many elementary schools enhance their classroom-based learning with Web-based instruction. They, too, take advantage of the plethora of resources and expertise now available to them on the Web. These may be in the form of individual exercises or activities, or in the use of entire courses for certain groups of students. When planning curricula for the elementary student population, it helps to review some of the resources already available and determine whether incorporating them into your environment is effective.

- Learning Planet http://www.learningplanet.com/
- Big Chalk http://www.bigchalk.com/
- Global Schoolhouse http://www.globalschoolhouse.org/
- Internet Education Resources http://www.cr.k12.ia.us/departments/tech/training/internet_resources.htm

Outside the United States, there are several other projects that provide resources and links to school age children around the world. These resources include newsletters, specific curriculum assistance for grammar school teachers, and the formation of networked organizations and experts. The majority of Web-based resources consist of links to networks of schools where one can then follow the links to specific projects within each school. Some links to these projects are:

- Project Happy Child News (UK) contains resources in several languages: http://www.happychild.org.uk/nvs/news/1999/index.htm
- School Cybersurfing Simplified, Reading University (UK): http://www.rdg.ac.uk/~esp99eca/home.html
- EduNet (Ireland): http://www.edunet.ie/whatis.html

- Australian Schools on the Web: http://www.edfac.unimelb.edu.au/Schools/aus_schools.shtml
- EduNet Japan: http://www.edunet.ie/links/japan.html

When teaching elementary children over the Web, the key population characteristics to keep in mind are age, maturity level, and specific goals of instruction. If the children are living in a city and exposed to technology regularly (e.g. television, computers, videos), then the entertainment value of instruction also becomes an issue.

Children already have very short attention spans (estimated at five to seven minutes). Thus instructional design must include graphics, motion, quick-pacing and changes in the *presentation* of the content. The content itself needs to be developed in brief chunks and each informational chunk presented in a variety of formats. Many designers make the mistake of developing content in a Web-based course that actually lessens the amount of content delivered in the course. This occurs because they are concentrating on entertainment values and incorporating change (through content changes) to keep the child's attention. It is vital to develop the same amount of content (or more) that has always been required for mastery of a topic; however, the presentation of the content is in smaller segments, with each fragment presented several times in different manners. This provides a means of drill and practice, review, and opportunities for acceleration or more depth for learning information while still maintaining the entertainment value and quick pacing.

Secondary students

Students choosing to participate in Web-based education at the secondary level have frequently earned above average achievement levels in the traditional class-room. They are taking advanced placement courses via distance education to fulfill college acceptance requirements. These students are motivated to learn because, for many of them, distance education is the only way to access the courses they need. Entwistle and Ramdsen (1983) found that distance students were intrinsically motivated, enjoyed learning for its own sake, and were actively involved with what they were learning. The researchers indicated that over 88 percent of these students planned to attend college.

The key attributes to remember about this group are that they maintain many of the characteristics that apply to learners of all ages. On the one hand, they are interested in learning and seem to become easily excited by new concepts. They want to understand the relationship of the topic to their real-world experience, and they wish to be viewed as intelligent, independent learners. On the other hand, they can become easily discouraged when things don't go well. As a developer, you should pay extra attention to design elements such as setting expectations, detailing learning objectives, supplying advanced organizers, presenting step-by-step instructions and examples, and above all providing encouragement and learning reinforcement.

Both traditional secondary schools and parents and students involved in home schooling frequently access the Web for additional curricula resources. Some interesting examples of these resources are below:

- Enhance your Curriculum http://ce.byu.edu/is/curriculum.htm
- Connecting high school students around the world with project-based studies: Lemvig Gymnasium, Denmark http://www.lemvig-gym.dk/english/profile.htm
- History and Social Science Web Resources http://www.ecnet.net/users/gdlevin/sstudies.html
- Writing and Language Arts Example http://www.wordsmith.org/
- SEED (Schlumberger Excellence in Educational Development) http://www.slb.com/seed SEED offers learners a real-world, real people context in which to develop their interest and excitement about science: http://www.1.slb.com/seed/

At-risk students

At-risk students include those who have exhibited learning disabilities, behavior problems, drug or alcohol abuse, or those who come from dysfunctional families. They are often considered a population that needs special assistance and would not perform well in the Web-based environment. As early as 1988, Bates found that televised instruction was especially useful to students who were struggling in school. Television worked because the visual medium allowed them to understand concepts through the use of concrete examples. Later studies found that offering remedial courses through a variety of distance education methods proved helpful to this population of students.

To date, there do not appear to be many Web-based courses offered to this at-risk population. However, there are several network sites designed to bring best practices and ideas together to begin to serve this population more effectively. An example of such a site is the IdeaDepot at http://www.ideapractices.org/ideadepot.htm

These students frequently come from poor environments, both rural and urban, with few personal or community support structures. These students are:

- Less likely to be exposed to the uses of technology.
- Less likely to have a home computer.
- Less likely to have well developed communication skills (written or oral).
- Easily discouraged.
- Need frequent positive reinforcement.
- Need increased time to perform learning tasks.
- Need increased opportunities to develop reasoning and higher-order thinking skills.
- Need assistance in developing study skills.
- More frequently suffer from test anxiety.

There are several successful projects that link at-risk students with mentors and tutors to build friendships and motivating relationships. These are usually through urban colleges or universities, which means a great number of potential students are being left out because of the nature of this format. In the future, this same mentoring and tutoring could be done over the Web and would be particularly promising with rural students who cannot easily access university or other organizational mentors/tutors available in urban environments.

Adult learners

Much has been written about adult learner characteristics and how to teach adults effectively. This book will only summarize some of the key characteristics of adult learners, and the implications for instructional design.

One way to describe how adults learn was developed by Malcolm Knowles during the 1970s. He called his theory "andragogy." Among the many tenets of adult learning, two basic aspects establish the foundation of Knowle's theory.

- Adults have a great deal of experience and knowledge upon which to build.
- Adults usually have specific learning goals in mind when they decide to continue their education.

Andragogy is on the constructivist side of the learning philosophy continuum. This means that learning is an internal (and interpretive) process of construction on the part of the learner, with guidance, assistance, and advice from the teacher. Moreover, adult learners expect to be able to use their learning in specific ways in the near future, if not immediately. One of the principles agreed on by most constructivists emphasizes that authentic activities, as opposed to activities that have no real-world relationship, are essential for adult learners. Therefore, if authentic learning is to occur, the instructional strategies used by teachers must encourage the construction of new knowledge and its integration into the learner's existing knowledge/experience base. A clear understanding of how adults learn will help us to develop and use appropriate instructional strategies.

The following assumptions (Imel, 1994) underlie Knowles's (1984) andragogical model:

- Adults tend to be self-directing.
- Adults have a rich reservoir of experience that can serve as a resource for learning.
- Since adults' readiness to learn is frequently affected by their need to know or do something, they tend to have a life-, task-, or problem-centered orientation to learning as opposed to a subject-matter orientation.
- Adults are generally motivated to learn by internal or intrinsic factors (such as helping their child with homework) as opposed to external or extrinsic forces (such as a raise in salary).

Selecting and applying instructional strategies based on an understanding of andragogy is an essential tool for effective online learning development and facilitation. Moving away from a focus on ourselves as teachers and focusing instead on the learner, we begin making the transition from the traditional knowledge transmission model to a facilitation model that enables us to involve students in their learning processes. In turn, we enable them to be more responsible for their own education, assist them with achieving their goals, and help them to apply their learning quickly to specific situations that are meaningful to them. Several instructional strategies have proven useful for adults. Table 2.1 provides a summary of the types of teaching strategies that relate to specific adult learner characteristics. The specific means to incorporate these teaching strategies into your course will be discussed in later chapters.

Planning and designing your Web-based access and interface based on student needs

The foundational technology that supports Web-based learning, as well as the interface (the look and feel) of that technology, can make a significant difference in how well the student learns. A teacher may design beautiful Web pages, excellent learning activities, and a dynamic interactive discussion. But if access to the Web pages is slow, the navigation varies from course to course, the use of the discussion board is confusing, or the learning activities are difficult to retrieve, then the learning becomes ineffective in spite of the modules instructional design. Identifying appropriate client and server hardware and software, as well as developing a good, consistent, shared structure and interface, should be one of the first steps in building your virtual classroom environment.

The technology elements you need to identify and implement effectively for your Web-based classroom include:

- Server hardware and software selection and configuration.
- Client hardware and software selection and configuration.
- Distribution and communication method for server and client.
- Institution/Department/Curricula/Course interface design.
- Security.
- Technical support.

To fully describe each element would require six additional books. To become an authority in each element would take years. Instead of trying to become an expert in all the elements, plan to assemble a team of specialists who are committed to the implementation of the virtual classroom environment. The requirements for each of the elements will be summarized in the following paragraphs.

Server hardware and software selection and configuration

The server hardware hosts the virtual environment. This hardware may vary in size from as small as a single personal computer in one office to as large as a UNIX box (e.g. SUN or DEC) or an array of boxes in a centralized computer department. It is wise to get the assistance of your administrative computing personnel to determine what needs you will have for hardware and what is the most cost-effective way to

Table 2.1 Teaching strategies for adult learner characteristics

Adult learner characteristic	Teaching strategy
Bring a rich reservoir of knowledge and experience that can serve as a resource for learning	Use your students as resources for yourself and for other students. Allow them to take a leadership role in the class – even to "teach" certain portions of the class to other students. Encourage dialogue that brings out their experiences. Use a reflection process for assignments (e.g. keeping journals, writing reflection papers, summarizing)
Possess established values, beliefs, and opinions that need an opportunity to be expressed and evaluated against the new knowledge	Take time to clarify student expectations of the course; permit debate and the challenge of ideas; be careful to protect minority opinions within the class; incorporate opposing opinions in assignments whenever possible
Expect to be treated as mature, thinking individuals and wish to be part of a community of like-minded learners	Treat questions and comments with respect; acknowledge contributions students make to the class; do not expect students to necessarily agree with your plan for the course. Develop collaboration projects by using group assignments to maintain interest, help develop a learning community, and facilitate students' application of higher-order thinking skills such as analysis, synthesis, and evaluation
Want to feel self-directed, with opportunities for review or more in-depth research as desired	Engage students in designing the learning process; expect students to want more than one medium for learning and to want control over the learning pace and start/stop times. Encourage the learner to go beyond the immediate course content, to discover and construct new knowledge. Instead, give options for additional research or study
Take a problem-centered approach to learning and desire application to the real-world environment in which they live/work	Show immediately how new knowledge or skills can be applied to current problems or situations; use participatory techniques such as case studies, role-playing, and problem-solving groups. Ask for examples of how it can be used in students' lives
Express less interest in survey (theory) types of courses and more interest in problem-solving and product creation	Focus on theories and concepts within the context of their applications to relevant problems; orient the course content toward direct applications rather than toward theory alone. Encourage implementation of theories in their work/life environment and then follow up with a reflective process to help in assimilation of the theory
Exhibit great variation in learning styles (individual differences increase with age, as does the desire to use a variety of styles to comprehend)	Use a variety of teaching materials and methods to take into account differences in style, time, types, and pace of learning (e.g. text, graphics, discussions, simulations, writing, direct application to their work/home environment)
Accept responsibility for their own learning if the subject is perceived as timely and appropriate	Establish peer study groups and incorporate peer reviews to encourage students to discuss their work. Provide a means for students to share their work with the entire class, such as creating a Web page to display their work

assist you. It may be that your virtual classroom can be run on existing hardware in the beginning and then moved to its own hardware as more courses are put online.

In most Web-based classrooms, the information disseminated via Web pages and the communication tools used in the class all reside on a single server computer. If there are hundreds of classes or thousands of students, then it is possible that several server computers will be connected together to support the Web-based environment. The server computer usually supports several software programs that are used in the virtual classroom. The most common programs in virtual classes currently are:

- E-mail, including mailing lists.
- Web pages.
- User authentication.
- Student tracking.
- Discussion board or bulletin board.
- Chat Room.
- Whiteboard.
- Student and Teacher File Management (upload/download/shared space).
- A course management system (CMS) like WebCT, Blackboard, or Top Class.

Whatever the configuration of software, the server's ability to deliver the tools speedily and without problems will have significant influence on the student's and teacher's experience and success in that virtual classroom.

In determining what configuration of hardware/software is required to meet your needs, discuss some of these questions with your technical personnel.

- How many classes do you intend to create and make available over the next two to three years?
- How many students (in total) do you anticipate in these classes over the next two to three years?
- What type of server access do you currently have available? Does it need to be enhanced?
- What operating system does the server use? Will it interface with the variety of systems anticipated?
- What type of speed does your server have?
- What type of connection do you expect your students to have (dial-up, cable, satellite, on campus or from home)?
- If the server is used for functions other than Web-based classes, how will that impact reliability and speed for students?
- What software is currently available on the server? Do you need to add new software? (Examples: FTP, real audio/video, chat, discussion board, whiteboard, CMS.)
- What type of support do you need for ensuring that this server will be as trouble-free and imperceptible as possible to the students and teachers in the virtual classroom?

Client hardware and software selection and configuration

The client hardware and software is that collection of computers and software that reside on the students' and teachers' individual systems – usually a desktop computer or laptop. It is this hardware and software that allow the teachers and students to access the virtual classroom. It is strongly advised that a recommended minimum client hardware/software configuration be mandated in order to avoid attempting to support too large a variety of computer types and software types. A typical virtual student or teacher *minimum* computer configuration today might be as follows:

- *Hardware*
  Pentium II or 266 MHz equivalent (Mac or PC)
  64 k RAM
  20 Gb hard disk drive
  CD-ROM drive
  HD floppy disk drive
  56 k modem
  Inkjet or laser printer
- *Software*
  Netscape Communicator 4.5 or Internet Explorer 5.0
  Microsoft Word 2000
  Microsoft Excel 2000
  Adobe Acrobat reader plug-in
  Real Player reader plug-in
  Shockwave plug-in
  Flash plug-in

Note that the minimum hardware specification is usually at least one year to eighteen months behind the most recent release. You don't want to be supporting old hardware, but you don't want to force everyone to upgrade to the latest version either.

It is wise to expect students and teachers to have a fairly recent version of the required software. Transferring files and reading Web pages are the most difficult things to support in the virtual environment. The closer students and teachers get to using the same software and versions the less help desk traffic you will experience.

Finally, it is important to identify any other peripherals that will be needed by your students and teachers. Some typical additional peripherals that may be needed are:

- Scanner.
- Video-camera.
- Pen drawing template.

Distribution and communication method for server and client

An essential part of the Web-based classroom is the distribution and storage of information among students and teachers. Usually, access to Web pages and to the course information and activities on the Web occurs via the institution's network (intranet). To maximize use of space and minimize the time required for access, it is important to carefully plan the types of content and communication that will occur, as well as the best way to store and manage that information. Pay particular attention to those resources that can be shared. Some questions to ask about shared resources include:

- Do you plan to share any course components or content information with other courses? For example, certain pictures and content developed on Abraham Lincoln may be used by a history course on the Civil War as well as by an overview history course on American history or another course on slavery and its impact in America.
- Do you foresee a need for students to communicate with each other among similar classes? For example, you may want to provide chat rooms or discussion boards that are shared by all students taking Algebra I, even though there may be several instructors or sections of students.
- Do you want to provide a virtual student lounge that any student may enter at any time? This may encourage the always important virtual community.
- Is it important for teacher information to be shared or reused from one course to the next (e.g. contact information, office hours, résumé)?
- Do you want a space for student information that can be accessed and redisplayed from one course to the next (e.g. a student Web page with background, contact information, etc.)?
- Do you want to build an image bank that can be accessed by many courses to alleviate searching for or recreating images that have already been produced?
- Do you want a single virtual resource center where students access videos, sound files, sample papers, etc., or do you want those resources kept separate for each course?
- Do you want to interface with other administrative databases? For example, do you want your Banner system to populate classes automatically based on registration? Do you want course grades to be transferred automatically to the registrar or to be mailed to students at the end of the course?
- Do you want some automatic system for notifying teachers of their assigned classes or notifying students of their approved schedule?
- Do you want an automatic system for providing user identification, password, and other course access information to students and teachers?

Answers to each of these questions will impact the design of the structure for your virtual environment. If you are selecting a CMS system, these questions should be a part of that selection. If you are creating your own system by selecting a variety of programs and tools, then these questions will help you determine what tools you need and what type of programming support you may need to interface the tools into one user-transparent system. Specific discussions of CMS systems are provided later in this chapter.

In addition to structural decisions about the location and distribution of information and resources in your virtual environment, you must also make decisions about distributing course materials and using other tools, including CDs, floppy disks, or faxes. How will these be distributed and how will they be referenced within the virtual course structure? For example, will you instruct the students to put in a CD to view a tutorial? Will you ask students to fax you information if they cannot provide it as an attachment (e.g. math students might have worked calculations by hand and not have a way to scan it to a file)?

You may also have non-electronic materials that need to be distributed such as textbooks, article packets, and video tapes. You need to determine how the students will request or obtain the non-electronic material. Will they request it via an online form? Will the materials be sent to them automatically when they register for the course? Will they interact with a student bookstore or library, and if so does that entity have online access?

Distribution is a key component of Web-based course delivery. It is also an issue that requires expertise both from technical personnel in computing and from educational personnel. Careful planning and discussion around this issue will make a significant difference in the ultimate successful implementation of your Web-based course delivery system.

Institution/department/curricula/course interface design

Once you have determined your hardware and software requirements and implemented your Internet structure for the virtual environment, you are ready to begin the interface design – the look and feel of your courses – that will represent your institution, department, and entire curriculum. The structure and design define the manner in which students and teachers will access and interact with information within your courses. A well designed appearance will make your site easier to navigate and will motivate and attract students. Even if you have elected to use a CMS system (e.g. WebCT, Blackboard) you will still want to spend time determining which features you wish to implement, how you want them presented, and if you will use a course template for all courses offered by your institution.

Interface design is an art that draws on the skills of many professionals: computer programmers, graphic designers, multimedia designers, and educators. Design is also a matter of taste and purpose. Many teachers would argue that a design that suits a chemistry class should be very different from a design for a music class. The key in interface design is to provide a common navigational system and to design a course template that provides common colors, headers and footers, yet allows the teacher freedom to include a variety of content types that meet the unique needs of his or her students. Questions to consider when planning your interface are:

- Do you want a single theme or metaphor for all courses or something different for each department/course/instructor?
- How will elements be placed on a page and in what order? For example, should every page begin with learning objectives, followed by an introduction, then required reading, instructor notes, and homework assignments?
- Where will the navigation be? In a frame to the left? On a home page? On top of each page? At the bottom of each page? Some combination of frames and internal navigation?
- Where will the internal and external page-specific links be located? Included within the text or image on a page? Listed under a "links" item? How can students save or bookmark links both internally and externally?
- What quality of icons or images do you want to use? It is important that the value remains consistent. In other words, if you are using photographs for images, you need to use photographs throughout. Do not mix clip art with photographs or line drawings.
- What type of contact and help information do you want to provide and how will it be accessed?

Define a theme or metaphor

To begin the interface design process, you should first review any current Web pages that are offered by your organization, then determine what part of that design should be repeated in the look-and-feel of your virtual classroom design. In effect, you want to develop a theme for your virtual environment. Themes range from a simple layout articulation such as "all print is black, headers are blue, and the background image is a notebook" to a complex metaphor that extends throughout your sites.

A common metaphor provides a graphical representation of your environment. In Figure 2.1, a virtual office serves as the Welcome page for all courses. The picture contains various elements hyperlinked for navigation. In this example, the student would click on the calendar to pop up a schedule of due dates and important class events. He or she would click on the book marked "home" to go to the course introduction, and click on the rocket to get technical support. Each book on the desk could be a different hyperlinked topic within a course or provide navigation to other activities (e.g. e-mail, chat, discussion boards, etc.). Whenever the student selected an icon, that icon would then be repeated on subsequent pages. For example, if the student selected the book marked "home" the introductory page would have the same book (perhaps opened) marked "home." All navigational footers would have the same set of books presented in the same manner. This type of metaphor or theme provides a defined look-and-feel for a course and sets up a consistent template from one page to the next, as well as from course to course. However, the metaphor and template do not limit the creativity of an instructor or course designer for including any type of content or activities he or she may wish to provide.

Figure 2.1 Virtual office graphic as welcome page

Define page types

Once you have defined and created a theme template, you should next define all the page types you will need in a typical virtual classroom environment and what elements are common to each and different in each. Depending on your design, these pages may be combined to form one page with internal links, or used separately. You may also elect to have each teacher define which pages are combined and which are separate. The key, again, is to ensure a consistent theme and navigation. A table of typical page types is shown in Table 2.2.

Create page templates

A page template is a skeleton Web page that contains most of the structure and components that form the presentation of information. Each new page is created by using an empty template and then providing the content for the new page. The template provides standard categories or elements that are needed on every page, such as the header, the body, and the footer.

- *The header* is everything that appears before the main content of the page. It usually includes a title, a graphic or institutional logo, and perhaps some navigation.
- *The body* contains the main content of the page and is usually unique for each particular page.
- *The footer* usually contains navigation links, including a Top of Page link, as well as the author of the page and the date the page was last modified. It often also contains some of the same information as the header.

Table 2.2 Typical page types

Page type	Description	Commonalities and differences
Home page or welcome page	Usually serves as an introduction to the course or curriculum. Should be colorful, inviting, interesting, and motivational.	Frequently the home page will also contain navigational links. The home page should be separate from the Syllabus. Because it is the first page seen by the student, it needs to be welcoming and encouraging.
Navigational page or index page	Introduces the structure of the course and offers quick links to important sections of the course. It may be offered as a separate page or part of a constant frame seen by the user. Make sure the links are listed separately somewhere so students don't have to go on a treasure hunt to find them.	The navigational information may be part of several other pages. It may be separated by a frame or integrated into pages. You might also select a combination wherein major category navigation is provided on the Index page and minor category navigation is provided within content or activity pages.
Calendar pages	Usually a graphical calendar used to show important dates within the course. It may include assignment due dates, course start and end dates, specific test dates, etc.	May not be part of the course at all. May be made available as a pop-up window or separate frame. May be integrated with other course pages.
Syllabus pages	Provides a course outline and specific instructions for taking the course and the expectations. Frequently includes due dates, assignments, and grading procedures.	Usually maintained as a separate page. May be shared by several course sections and, thus, several instructors and students.
Content pages	The primary page structure within a course and may contain all the other course-related pages (activities, lecture notes, study guides) as well. This page should be the least structured as it changes significantly from course to course. If content is provided in a frame, make sure the frame can be opened as a separate page for students who want to print it.	The only template elements are usually a header and footer style and perhaps specific background selection. These pages should allow for the greatest latitude in individual design and use.

Table 2.2 (*continued*)

Page type	Description	Commonalities and differences
Activity pages	May be assignments, links, special interactions designed for the course (e.g. role-plays, simulations, home-work specifics). Sometimes activity pages are divided into Web-based activity and non-Web-based activity, such as reading the textbook.	Specific design elements for activity types should be consistent. For example, a consistent icon for chat, discussion board, whiteboard, role-play, reading, etc. However, as with content pages, these pages should allow for a great deal of latitude in individual design of the activities.
Lecture notes or instructor notes pages	Different from content pages in that these pages generally provide static information. They may be presented in a sequential structure with some navigational links forward and backward or to outside resources.	Frequently the Notes pages are included as part of the content pages. The key is to have consistent headers and footers and for navigation to be easy to follow. Usually text based, it helps to have a template for colors of heads, subheads, indentations, etc. just as you would in a wordprocessed document.
Study guide pages	Used as the primary source for describing how the student might best master the material in the course. Often used as a resource in preparing for tests, labs, homework, etc.	Frequently incorporated as part of the content pages or the syllabus. May be a summary page of several assignments contained in content pages. Should provide common headers and footers with the rest of the course and be easy to find and navigate.

General design considerations

The following considerations are important in creating your Web pages.

- *Content is king.* The design of your interface should not distract from the content. For example, too many animated features, blinking words, explosions of color distract from the content by drawing the reader's eye away from what is important. This often results in the user missing key points or being overwhelmed by the flashing and unable to navigate your pages effectively. It also slows down page processing for less powerful computers or dial-up modem connections.
- *Follow the KISS rule (Keep It Simple, Silly).* Keep your page layout simple and clean. Do not overload your page with graphical dividers, multicolored bullets, and backgrounds that make the text difficult to read. Have someone who

knows nothing about your content try to read and understand your Web page. Is it legible? Are the font sizes good for reflecting the content? Are the colors inviting?

- *Keep consistent navigation.* Consistency means predictability, which will make it possible for users to become familiar with the common "behaviors" of your site and be able to predict how to perform tasks and find their way around. Changing the navigation from one page to the next, or one course to the next, will only confuse people.
- *Use color cautiously.* Colors provide a simple method to indicate purpose, tasks, events, or to designate a grouping of information. Correct use of colors can improve the legibility of a site. Poor use of colors can destroy a site. The rule of thumb is to use no more than four colors in a single page and no more than seven colors for an entire course.
- *Choose graphics that portray meaning.* Graphics are a key component of good Web pages. They are used to give visual cues for meaning. Good graphic icons are often easier for users to remember than words. However, poor graphic icons cause confusion and lose meaning. As stated previously, you must also select the *value* of your graphics and remain consistent. If you are using line drawings, then maintain the same graphic *value* throughout. Do not mix clip art with line drawings or with high quality photographs.

There are a number of sites on the Web with information about Web page design. One nicely presented site with good examples is: http://www.usask.ca/education/coursework/skaalid/textindex.htm.

Limitations: what you can't control in design

Even if you design the "perfect" Web page, it is probable that 50 percent of your users won't see it the way you designed it. Three common technology limitations affect what the users actually see: speed, resolution, and color values.

- *Speed.* The speed at which the user downloads your page is dependent on many factors beyond your control: users' connection speed, the time of day they connect, the speed of their computer, and the number of people simultaneously connecting to your site. For this reason you need to keep graphics small and few (or linked). It is wise to keep them to 50 k or less in file size.
- *Resolution.* Computer monitor resolutions range from 640 × 480 to 1,280 × 1,024. If you design for the highest resolution, those using a lower resolution are at a disadvantage. The key is to design the page so that it looks good at any resolution. Test it in each environment to make sure it is still legible. This is particularly important if you are using frames, border backgrounds, or tiling that may look strange in some resolutions.
- *Colors.* Depending on the user's computer, current configuration, and monitor, the number of colors that will be displayed will vary from monochrome (rare) to 24 bit (millions of colors). It is wise to design colors for the average of 8–16

bit displays. Additionally, users can change default colors in the browser for links, backgrounds, and text elements that may override your selection. Stick to the rule of no more than four colors per page and seven colors per course, and try to stay within certain values and hues so that the colors will still look good together even on lesser displays.

Security

Most systems allow you to implement various levels of security. Your specific needs and the amount of integration you plan in your virtual environment will determine the level of security that is appropriate for your organization. The key is to find a strategic balance between security and accessibility. Too much security makes life difficult for even authorized users, whereas not enough security makes your system an easy target for electronic hackers and plagiarists. Some questions to consider about security are:

- Do you want courses password-protected and available only to specific students or groups of individuals? Or do you want them available to anyone on the Web?
- Do you want student and teacher authentication? If so, at what level?
- Do you want to track use by authorized users?
- Are you concerned about student access to inappropriate material?
- Do you need protection against viruses?
- Will you allow users to run scripts on your server? If so, will that be only in a defined space that does not allow access to other systems?
- If you are running your Web-based classrooms on a server also used for organization administration, do you want protection to ensure the Web-server section does not have access to the administration section?

As with the distribution topic previously, it is important to have your computing personnel involved in this decision-making process. Below are a number of resources you may consider when making security decisions.

Inappropriate material screening

Elementary schools are often worried about allowing students access to the Internet because of the potential for accidental viewing of inappropriate material. Frequently, a search on a key word will turn up something unexpected (e.g. pornographic sites). In the near future it is possible that these sites will be easily identifiable and filtered, as there is a movement for adding URL extensions to the growing number of Internet sites. In the meantime, you can purchase client software that will screen sites. Some of the popular programs are:

- Net Nanny http://www.netnanny.com/
- CyberPatrol http://ww.cyberpatrol.com/
- CyberSitter http://www.solidak.com/

Another way of screening is to have all monitored browsers send their URL requests through a proxy system that checks whether the request is appropriate. The proxy computer that handles the requests maintains a list of banned sites or search words. For an example, see the site at http://www.bess.net/. If you elect to do this and build your own system of banned sites or search words, you may wish to subscribe to a rating service like Shepherd at http://www.shepherd.net.

Checking server security

No system connected to a network is completely secure. However, there are programs that will probe your server for security weaknesses and then report those weaknesses to you. Some programs will also provide a tutorial on how to resolve those weaknesses. You can find a set of free utilities that will do this at http://www.fish.com/satan/.

In addition, there are software packages that will audit your security system to check for holes, and packages that will check to see whether files have been altered since the last time a program was run. Tripwire is a file alteration checker: ftp://coast.cs.purdue.edu/edu/pub/COAST/Tripwire/. A popular site for auditing packages is ftp://ftp.cert.org/pub/tools/cops/.

Secure server protocols

If you have done any shopping on the Web, you have probably encountered secure server sites. These are sites that encrypt, or scramble, communication between the browser and server so that it cannot be read by an unauthorized third party. Typically, this is used to protect confidential information, such as your credit card number.

In the virtual classroom environment, this same technology is particularly valuable for all the online support services you may offer distance students – registration, tuition payment, grade access, financial aid information, exam papers, etc. This same secure type of encryption is available to you and may be installed on your Web server. The most widely used system recognized today is Secure Socket Layer (SSL), which was developed by Netscape. See http://home.netscape.com/newsref/std for details on this system. To use this system, you must obtain an HTTP server that supports it. This server extension varies, depending on your operating system and your geographic location.

- Netscape's Commerce Server for NT/UNIX http://www.netscape.com
- Commerce Builder for Windows NT http://www.ifact.com/
- For Apache inside the United States try Stronghold http://www.us.apache-ssl.com/
- For Apache outside the United States try Apache-SSL http://www.algroup.co.uk/Apache-SSL

Remember that all these systems do is encrypt the information traveling between the browser and the server; they do not improve the security of the server. You must still ensure server security through the number of other tools suggested in this chapter.

Password checkers

The most common security weakness is password breaking. If passwords are not well chosen, they can be guessed easily. Also, hackers build programs that go through common passwords based on people's names, addresses, phone numbers, social security numbers, birth dates, etc. It is wise to give all users specific guidelines when selecting passwords. Here is a list you may wish to offer your students when choosing their password:

- The password must not be found in a dictionary.
- The password must be a minimum of eight characters, including a mix of numbers and letters as well as upper and lower-case letters (e.g. McV249xl).
- Do not use the same password for all machines to which you have access.
- If you must write down your password, put the note in a secure location.
- Do not share your password with anyone and make sure nobody can see you typing the password.

Another alternative to allowing users to select their own password is to generate one for them. However, though this is secure, it is often frustrating for users, because the password then has no personal meaning for them. Again, this is an area where security and ease of use must be balanced in some way.

Once users have selected passwords and you have stored them in a password file, you may wish to run a utility to check whether the passwords are secure. One such utility for Unix systems is called "Crack." You can find it at ftp://ftp. cert.org/pub/tools/crack. If the Crack program guesses a password, it reports the name of the user to you. This user can then be told to choose a better password.

Scripts

Scripts are programs that access the server resources, usually to store temporary variables, pass information, or make a page or activity interactive. For example, the drop-down menu you may see on Web page navigational tools is a script that passes information between the browser and server – information such as where your cursor is positioned, what item you have selected, the last page you accessed, where you want to go, etc. The use of scripts by developers can make navigation easier and provides a number of important processes on Web pages (e.g. forms, animations, various interactions). However, scripts run by unauthorized users or by those who may not be adept at their implementation can cause havoc on your server. Furthermore, savvy persons can sometimes use scripts to circumvent security precautions on UNIX systems. For example, they could create programs that would allow them to perform tasks that exceed their privileges, such as copying or deleting other users' files.

Unfortunately, it is not easy to simply restrict all users from running scripts. In addition to the benefits of scripts mentioned above, you might have users who need to run them for classes (e.g. computer science students). One solution is to provide a separate machine, or protected space, for users where scripts can be tested for learning purposes.

Viruses

Viruses are programs that attach themselves to other programs and to data files. They can then have a negative effect on the server and on individual personal computers. The effect can range from a "harmless" message displayed to the user when the program is opened (e.g. "School sucks") to the deletion or corruption of files and programs. Some of the worst viruses can delete or corrupt the contents of your entire hard drive. Viruses can be found on most major operating systems and frequently occur in wordprocessed documents. Many times a user will have a virus and pass it on without even knowing it.

To avoid acquiring viruses, always use a virus-checking program to verify that applications and files are virus-free before students download or upload them to your server. Anti-viral software often encompasses two very separate functions – virus scanning and virus cleaning. Most of the top applications integrate these dual functions. It is wise to also require that remote students have a virus program resident on their computers. Two top virus scanning programs are:

* McAfee http://www.mcafee.com
* Norton http://www.symantec.com

There are a number of other virus packages, some that run on operating systems not supported by McAfee or Norton, and others that are freeware. For one review of the top packages, check Stroud's Virus Scanner Review at http://cwsapps.txcyber.com/32virus-reviews.html.

Education is the best preventative in your fight against viruses. Consider providing a guide sheet to students and teachers that clearly describes how viruses are acquired and how they can prevent them and eradicate them. Virus hoaxes also abound on the Web and can spread quickly through student e-mails. One way to educate users about hoax e-mails is to point them to http://www.Vmyths.com/.

Technical support

In a traditional classroom, students have the teacher to assist them with problems. If they don't understand a word, the teacher is there to give a synonym. In a lab environment, the student may ask the teacher how to troubleshoot a computer problem or the teacher may have a lab assistant to help him or her when something goes wrong. In elementary schools, teachers frequently have assistants who may help photocopy materials, prepare video recorders and televisions, and maintain the rooms in general. A Web-based classroom, on the other hand, leaves both students and teachers to their own devices in troubleshooting difficulties and provides new challenges for interaction when something goes wrong. Technical support decisions need to be made early in the Web-based environment development process. You need to answer the following questions:

- Who will be responsible for the server software and hardware installation and maintenance?
- Who will be responsible for the network infrastructure, adding or deleting users, and keeping the network available twenty-four hours a day, seven days a week?
- Who will provide training to students, teachers, and other support personnel in the use of the Web-based technology?
- Who will be responsible for answering questions and resolving problems for students, teachers, and other support personnel? Who will be responsible for developing and maintaining FAQs on the server?
- How will technical support be accessed? By phone? Through e-mail? By having to physically track someone down?
- What hours will technical support be available?

There are a number of options an institution may select in order to provide effective technical support in all these areas:

- Using in-house personnel who may already exist and/or supplementing in-house personnel with new hires dedicated to the Web-based classroom environment.
- Using a combination of contract employees and in-house personnel.
- Using student workers (e.g. senior computer science students).
- Contracting all technical support, including Web server hosting and security, to an outside vendor.

All of these options have their pros and cons, depending on your institution's needs, budget, and current capabilities. As discussed early in this chapter, the key is to form a team of experts when making all the decisions about the technical aspects of implementing a Web-based learning environment.

Selecting or creating a course management system (CMS)

There are a number of tools available today for assisting educators and administrators in building and maintaining Web-based learning environments. The question for many educators is "Which tool should I use?" Of course, there is no one answer that meets everyone's needs. The best approach is to read reviews of tools and then to test out three or four tools by actually putting up the same class, using each tool. For comparisons performed by other universities you may wish to begin your search by accessing the following sites:

- Marshall University's Comprehensive site: http://www.marshall.edu/it/cit/Webct/compare/comparison.html
- University of Wisconsin Comparison: http://fdc.uwsuper.edu/comp.html
- University of Wales Comparisons: http://www.jtap.ac.uk/reports/htm/jtap-041.html#_Toc463843848

We began this chapter by assessing student needs. Whether you are designing a course, selecting Web-based CMS tools, determining server requirements, or facilitating a class, the student is ultimately at the center of the discussion. By assessing these needs at the beginning of your planning process, you will be better equipped to answer the questions that lead to a choice of tools in the Web-based learning environment that works best for your organization.

3 Building support systems

In a systems approach to building a Web-based learning environment, it is necessary to remember all of the student and faculty support components that comprise the education organization. Determining the changed roles and requirements for each of these components affects all departments and administrative levels of the institute. Some components often neglected in the planning process are:

- Course registration.
- Grades and transcript transmittal.
- Help Desk (computer technical support, hardware and software).
- Research (library).
- Advising (personal and academic counseling).
- Tutoring.
- Textbook distribution.
- Marketing.
- Alumni associations.

Regardless of their position in the organization, it is imperative that all staff understand and value the nature of distance education and particularly the needs of Web-based learners. Since few people in an educational organization have had experience with Web-based learning, all staff should receive an orientation that conveys a student's perspective on this environment. They must appreciate and have a plan to alleviate the difficulties learners may experience.

It is important to have all staff participate in some type of *online* course in addition to any face-to-face presentations you may give. The course should minimally include student stories, practice with the communication tools Web-based students use, and some type of group activity that encourages plan development for individual departments or service sections. Specific change elements to consider in building support systems are discussed throughout this chapter along with technical considerations for building each of those elements.

Course registration

Foremost, Web-based students need to have a way to register without coming to the campus. This registration should minimally include the ability to select courses and receive confirmation of registration via the Web. This may be handled as simply as an e-mail interface to specific contact personnel or as complexly as creating Web-based form processing that adds students to a Banner system database and automatically responds to their e-mail when the registration is confirmed. In addition to Web-based registration, it is important to include other contact options such as telephone registration capabilities, contact phone numbers, and institutional addresses. For those students who are new to the Web, or who are experiencing technical difficulties, it is important to provide alternatives to the Web-based interface.

In addition to specific registrar capabilities, it is essential to also afford navigation to other departments that interact regularly with the registration office. For example, the bursar's office may be part of the registration confirmation process. Also, financial aid, student transcript processing, and the university catalog may need to be linked with the registration process. Prior to planning your Web-based registration capabilities, take time to fully analyze how a campus-based student interacts with various departments and be sure to provide those same capabilities to your distance students.

Example of an automated process with a Web interface

Maggie registers for a class. The following automatic events occur:

- Student Information System (SIS) notifies the campus system that student has registered.
- Maggie is added to teacher's group e-mail list for each class.
- Maggie is granted access to the following electronic information and communication areas.
  - Course resources for the class
  - Secure classroom chat
  - Class message boards
  - Syllabus and course FAQs
- An e-mail is sent to Maggie confirming her registration and access

Grades and transcript transmittal

Just as in building the electronic interface for registration, it is important for Web-based students to have easy electronic access to their grades and transcripts. Grades and transcripts are the elements that students worry about the most. Students are concerned about getting proof of their participation in education and training. They need this proof for certifications, financial reimbursements, and for final degrees. The ability to easily view grades and transcripts on an ongoing basis is necessary to a Web-based education system; it benefits traditional students as well. As with the registration process, such access may be made available as easily as providing e-mail contacts or as elaborately as providing individual, password-protected viewing of grades and transcripts on the Web. Several CMS systems offer capabilities for the viewing of grades during the class. A transcript viewing system may need to be developed that specifically interfaces with your registration department. Some examples of effective implementations of these functions can be viewed at the following college and university Web sites:

*   http://onestop.umn.edu/Grades/index.html
*   http://Webstar.nova.edu/
*   http://www.clms.le.ac.uk/WWW/HTML%20Pages/Students/student_access. html

Of course, there are software packages that will handle much of this for you. In the K-12 environment two products are frequently mentioned: Open District and K12 Planet, both available from Chancery Software: http://www.chancery.com/. Open District is a Web-based, district-level, student management system that aggregates data from all the school sites and quickly generates reports based on fresh, accurate data. K12 Planet is a secure Web site which parents and students use to see their latest grades, attendance, and details of homework assignments. Data are automatically drawn from the school's SIS system, requiring no double data entry on the part of school staff.

In higher education, a product that provides a variety of secure electronic access models is Campus Pipeline, http://www.campuspipeline.com/. This provides a system divided into administrative services, course services, study and information tools, and career services. All are integrated within the institution's Web site and provide single authentication access to students and staff. There are probably several other similar systems on the market. An example of the type of integrated services you want to purchase is described below in three subcategories.

*   *Administrative services.* Online access to registration, transcripts, grades, and personal information that you determine should be made available.
*   *Course services.* Applications that can provide a virtual extension of the classroom with a variety of online academic tools, including secure chat and message boards. If you use an existing CMS system, you want it to integrate with your overall Web presence. It is possible that these course services (e.g. a message board) are implemented for the entire student body, such as a virtual student lounge.
*   *Research and library tools.* An integrated application that will augment your organization's online library resources, including links with an array of Internet-based academic research tools and guides. This would also be the location to integrate tutoring resources.

Help Desk (computer technical support, hardware and software)

The purpose of instituting a Help Desk is to provide technical and educational services for faculty, staff and students. If online education delivery is a new addition to your institution, faculty and students are likely to have lots of questions. A well organized, friendly Help Desk can be essential to establishing your program. Most organizations have found that combining this support in a centralized location is the most efficient and cost-effective. A central location ensures that all personnel receive the same training and capitalizes on the sharing of information and resources. However, depending on the size and structure of your institution, another viable alternative is to support traditional students and online students separately or to have a Help Desk established in each department or division.

A Help Desk is much more than the maintenance of computing facilities. In fact, frequently the installation and maintenance is housed with facilities rather than with computing support. The Help Desk's primary responsibility is to provide technical assistance and troubleshooting. In order to do this efficiently, it is important to have some way in which to maintain a database of potential problems and fixes. This database then acts as an expert system and is accessed whenever a new call comes into the center. As with most things in technology, there is also software available to automate this process. A nice site for information on software, publications, and other resources is at Help Desk.Com, http://www.helpdesk.com/. Three popular packages are:

- Aegis http://www.abacus-systems.com/
- Track It http://www.blueocean.com/demo/welcome.html
- HelpSTAR http://www.helpstar.com/downloads/

Though software/hardware support is the primary focus of most Help Desks, you can also enhance problem prevention with a regular offering of education regarding computer use. Additionally, any information that you can provide to the Web will help to lessen the number of calls you experience. Some good examples of Help Desk pages are below:

- Portland State University http://www.helpdesk.pdx.edu/
- University of Tasmania http://www.educ.utas.edu.au/techservices/
- University of Wisconsin http://helpdesk.doit.wisc.edu/
- University of Victoria http://helpdesk.uvic.ca/

Another alternative to providing Help Desk support within your organization is to contract that support to a separate entity. Several commercial CMS developers also offer Help Desk support for your students and staff. They promise round-the-clock support using their centralized staff. Students and faculty call a toll-free number. Depending on your institutional needs, your in-house expertise, and your budget, using a contracted Help Desk service may be the most cost-effective solution. It is particularly handy for organizations that are just beginning to offer online courses, or those who have implemented a haphazard plan of online delivery and have discovered that they need outside assistance to move to the next level. One company that offers this type of support service, along with its course development and management tools, is Connected Learning Network, http://connectedlearning.net/. It provides the service in Europe and the United States, as well as Australia and Asia.

Research

A key component in Web-based distance education is the student's ability to obtain information and research materials. The student's foremost resource for this is a library. Imagine the following scenario. Dr Lynch has just assigned a research project for her education students with a due date in three weeks. As the project requirements are being read on her Web page, Hans in Regensburg makes a mental note to go to the university library and begin his research in the stacks of the well appointed educational resources. At the same time, Michele in rural Oregon wonders how she will find a library with this material. Her local community library certainly does not provide access to several of the education journals required for the project and it is a three-hour drive to the closest major university library. Finally, Cheryl, in the outback of Australia, begins to panic. For her, the closest library is two hours away by plane.

Though the worldwide dimension of this scenario may not match your institution, such situations are not uncommon. Many institutions serve rural learners or adult learners who may be very mobile. Your learner may be taking a course at home, or while on a business trip anywhere in the world. Though some students have access to a community library or small college library, often the holdings are limited or dated. The effectiveness of library services provided to online students can be a significant factor in students' success. It is for this reason that accreditation bodies in the United States have begun evaluating the library resources provided for distance students. These electronic resources or accessibility to such resources have become a key factor in accreditation of Web-based programs.

Librarians have been working aggressively to educate administrators and faculty to the realities and shortcomings of life online. They know that online catalogs, databases, electronic journals, newspapers, and library Web sites are important assets for serving students and faculty who study and teach at a distance. But current electronic resources constitute only a fraction of the services necessary to support academic programs, which also rely on face-to-face reference and instructional services and access to extensive print and otherwise non-digital collections. This means that, in addition to Web-based media, libraries must be prepared to mail and fax materials to students and to rely heavily on interlibrary loan mechanisms. This becomes even more critical when serving students across state and country borders.

Librarians also know that the Web, touted by the popular media and some educators as a free worldwide library, falls woefully short of that goal. The nitty-gritty issues of document delivery, interlibrary loan, access to licensed electronic materials, and instruction belie the warm, fuzzy idea that "information wants to be free," or that it's easy to find on your own through a Web search engine. Now, more than ever, library and information professionals have become activists for their services, inserting themselves into the development process of distance-based programs, poised to challenge their institutions on the quality and equitability of services that support these programs.

It is necessary for the educational institution to make a commitment to monitor the library's supporting role in the growth and development of distance and off-campus electronic programs. It means working closely with a library's program managers and departmental staffs to examine how existing services can be modified and new services developed to support distance-based communities. Increasingly, the titles "outreach information services librarian" and "electronic and distance education librarian" are appearing in job advertisements in the professional press. To be truly successful, librarians in these positions need the close support of a wide variety of staff, from instructional services librarians to library Webmasters, to document delivery specialists to site librarians out in the field.

Kirk and Bartelstein (1999: 41) provide an accurate description of such library services in their study of Central Michigan University.

> At Central Michigan University (CMU), seven full-time professional librarians based in Mount Pleasant, MI, Falls Church, VA, and metro Detroit provide reference, referral, and instruction to adult undergraduate and graduate students enrolled in extended learning programs in more than 70 locations in the United States, Canada, and Mexico. The off-campus library services librarians target research-based courses and travel regularly to remote classroom sites to provide in-person instruction. In addition to the librarians, a staff of five manages all aspects of document delivery and includes a copyright specialist who assists faculty in obtaining necessary permissions. Students and administrators in CMU's College of Extended Learning see library services as an invaluable aspect of distance programs. "The library component is a major marketing tool for the college, and they use it as such," said Connie Hildebrand, offcampus librarian, whose responsibilities include the western United States and international locations.

Librarians must also play an instructional role for students in Web-based learning. Teaching library users the skills required to locate, evaluate, and use information appropriately is important when more and more students are relying on the Web for information and research. It is particularly important for students to receive instruction on evaluating Web sites. Too many students make the assumption that if information is presented on the Web it must be accurate and backed by research.

In addition, as many Web-based programs are aimed at adults who want to further their education without excessive disruptions to their already full lives, these adults are often older returning students who may be insecure about their library skills or lack experience in using the new technologies. Special attention to the needs of these returning students will significantly enhance their opportunities for success in this new learning environment.

As with the previous examples of support, it is also possible that your institution does not need to provide this alone. Some institutions have chosen to partner with larger, established universities and use their electronic library services. For example,

Walden University (a school offering only online curricula) has no home campus or library services of its own; it contracts with Indiana University to provide staff, services, and resources to support Walden students and faculty. This allows Walden to offer appropriate services to its own population without having to build from the ground up. It also provides Indiana with a laboratory for crafting services to a distance-based patron group and brings revenue into the university libraries. This mutually beneficial approach stands in marked contrast to institutions, such as the University of Phoenix, that send their students out to find what they may at local public and academic libraries.

Some academic institutions are working within their communities to provide electronic library services at the local and community library level as well. One such example is Nova Southeastern University, a private undergraduate and graduate school with both traditional and Web-based degree programs. Since beginning its Web-based degree programs, Nova has provided excellent electronic library services. It not only subscribed to a plethora of online databases and full-text journals but also made librarians available via e-mail, telephone, and fax. Students reported turnaround times from as little as two hours to as much as two weeks when extensive materials need to be mailed to the student's home, with the average being a forty-eight-hour turnaround. Nova Southeastern University is now entering into an agreement to provide library services not only to its academic community but also to its local community (Broward County). This may serve as a model for sharing resources, costs, and expertise between public and private entities. http://www.nova.edu/library/nsulibs.htm

The University of Louisville also furnishes excellent library support and provides an integration model that works particularly well. It incorporates library educational services into the structure of the course via the professor's home Web page and any printed course-related materials. As the students become more information-literate through the use of resources accessible via the professor's home page, they are introduced to the broader world of information at their fingertips through links on the library's pages.

Edge and Edge (1998) articulated some of the important principles incorporated into the University of Louisville's Library Support for Distance Education Program as:

- Centralization of access.
- Immediacy of access.
- Rapid turnaround time for remote delivery.
- Empowerment of students to access information and to perform their own research on a self-service basis.

At a minimum, your library needs to focus on three areas of importance in supporting Web-based students – information literacy, reference services, and document delivery.

- *Information literacy*. Learning depends not only on classroom instruction and dialogue but also on the student's ability to locate and analyze information. The library needs to enhance students' ability to retrieve and evaluate the source of information needed for their course work (and for lifelong learning) on a self-service basis and to foster the belief that information literacy is a necessary component of any education experience.

- *Reference services*. Reference services must be sufficient so that students at remote locations can identify resources on a topic of their choice. These services should include provision of access to electronic databases for literature searches to determine books and journal articles relevant to course content. These resources must also be available to students and faculty on a self-service basis via their computer access, wherever that may be. It is not enough to offer computer access only on campus. Furthermore, the reference services should make a reference librarian available for consultation through a variety of methods (e-mail, toll-free phone number, message board, etc.). One example of this implementation might be a link on the library home page that provides the option of sending a question directly to the reference librarian associated with distance education support.
- *Document delivery*. Once students or faculty members have located a desired book or article, it is imperative that the delivery of that material be made quickly. Again, realizing that Web-based students may not be located anywhere near the institution, it is important for the specifically identified library materials to be delivered in the shortest possible time. Certainly, the subscription to full-text databases assists in this matter. Also, library staff have the option of copying and mailing or faxing material that they hold in their collection. However, as pointed out previously, frequently the material requested is not available or deliverable in digital format, nor is it available in the library's collection. In this instance, the goal needs to be to obtain the material from any place in the world and deliver it to students in their homes or workplaces.

Document delivery services should include:

- Access via the Web to selected databases (including some with full-text journal articles).
- Access to required readings placed on course reserve by distance education professors provided electronically on a self-service basis for items available in full-text or scanned into machine-readable form and delivered upon request via fax or mail for items not available in electronic format.
- Retrieval of books from the library's collection (including charging and delivery of books to students' homes via first-class mail).
- Retrieval and photocopying of journal articles held in the library's collection, and subsequent delivery of the articles to students via mail or fax.
- Retrieval of material in microfiche format for delivery to students via fax, e-mail, or home mail delivery. It is *not* sufficient to mail microfiche to students, as they may not have access to a reader.
- Retrieval from other libraries via the interlibrary loan system of books not held in the library's collection. Again these books should be delivered to the students' homes via first-class mail.

Advising (personal and academic counseling)

Educational advising services vary from campus to campus. Students may be assigned to specific advisors, or to a professor who becomes their advisor/mentor throughout their degree program; other times, advising is handled by a combination of clerical personnel and trained counselors. Whatever your means of providing advising services, you must determine how you will provide that same level of service to your Web-based students. Requiring students to come to the campus and meet with an advisor is unrealistic, as is merely providing pages of information on a Web site. You must provide a way for Web-based students to have the same access of one-to-one contact with an advisor that is provided for campus-based students. The two easiest ways to provide this access are via e-mail and/or toll-free telephone.

Much of the static information advisors offer can be provided on Web pages linked to the school advising offices. These may be set up as Frequently Asked Questions (FAQs) or individual information objects, or searchable objects. Whatever format you select, make sure it is easy to find and easy to understand. Some of the information you want to be sure to include on these static pages is:

- School programs – both general programs and specific majors.
- The application process.
- How to be a competitive applicant.
- Program calendars – start dates, end dates, holidays, test dates.
- Wait lists for entry to programs.
- Entrance requirements.
- Upgrading status, e.g. from no declared major to a specific major.
- Transcripts.
- Tuition costs.
- Pre-test or placement test information.
- Applying for transfer credit.
- Articulation agreements for transfer credit between schools.

In addition to the dissemination of advising information there are a number of communication tools you can use to facilitate the student advising process.

- Establish an advising message board open at the beginning of each term and/or during registration periods. This message board may link with many of the FAQ pages mentioned above, but it also provides a mechanism for students' general questions to be addressed.
- Offer electronic advising office hours (via chat) when students may "drop by" to ask questions and know they will receive an immediate response. If possible, also offer opportunities for participation in non-public chat rooms to ensure privacy.
- Provide a link with an advising "drop box" where students may ask an individual question with the guarantee of a response within forty-eight hours.

- Grant direct e-mail and telephone access to specified advisors for one-to-one conversations. This is particularly important in models where each student is assigned a specific advisor.

Because many staff will be new to advising via electronic methods, it is wise to require some communications training of your Web-based advisors. Electronic advising involves the use of written communication, instead of voice communication, so it is prudent to evaluate advisor skills in this area. Attention to the use and potential abuse of written language, clarity, and awareness of the potential for misinterpretation should be primary topics. Decisions about the formality expected in Web-based communication, the use of emoticons, and the potential liability of written promises should also be covered.

Links to some advising Web Page examples:

- University of Wisconsin Advising Toolkit http://www.wisc.edu/advise/
- Okanagan University College http://www.ouc.bc.ca/advising/
- Advising via e-mail at Wichita State University http://business.twsu.edu/advising.html
- Athabasca University http://www.athabascau.ca/html/services/advise/advise1.htm

Tutoring

Like advising, tutoring services are often overlooked with Web-based students. Many colleges and universities provide some type of campus-based tutoring services. These may be supplied via a teaching and learning center, through the library, or through special university services. Often tutors are advanced students or graduate students being paid as campus resources. If you provide tutoring services to your campus-based students, you must also provide those same services to your distance students. Again, these services are best provided via the Web.

In addition to e-mail and message boards for questions and answers, tutoring services may also use all the tools afforded professors and instructors. It is possible that tutors or departments would build entire "courses" for tutoring. For example, you might use your CMS system and have an open login for all pre-algebra math courses. Within this tutoring course, several tutors may be available – each with individual links, examples of problem sets, and e-mail contacts. Alternatively, individual tutors may wish to create their own Web presence that fits their specific tutoring needs.

Because tutoring can be so individualized, it is important to allow tutors to have use of all the tools of a CMS system – e-mail, message boards, Web pages, whiteboards, chat rooms, and shared student work spaces. Of particular use to the tutoring environment is the electronic whiteboard. This may most closely approximate sitting next to a student with a piece of paper and being able to draw diagrams, work problems, and circle important elements of an assignment.

As with advising services, it is important for the tutor not only to provide one-to-one asynchronous services, such as e-mail, but also to offer real-time services via chat office hours or whiteboard problem-solving sessions. Also, it is important to train tutors in the same communication skills regarding writing and misinterpretation. Both language and cultural differences, in addition to the already stressful environment of tutoring, can play a significant role in these written communications. Therefore, it is wise to provide some anticipatory training prior to implementing any full-scale tutoring program.

Examples of online tutoring implementations:

- Online Tutoring Skills Web site by Heriot-Watt University and the Robert Gordon University in the United Kingdom http://otis.scotcit.ac.uk/
- University of Colorado http://onlinetutor.cu.edu/
- Kingwood College http://kcWeb.nhmccd.edu/programs/cybercol/onlinetutoring. htm
- Weber State University (automated writing and math tutoring) http://wsuonline. Weber.edu/tutoring/academic.htm
- Teacher Education Tutoring http://www.3ked.co.uk/
- Long Beach City College http://clas.lbcc.cc.ca.us/OnlineTutoring/index.html

Textbook distribution

The normal way for students to obtain textbooks is to go to a campus bookstore, look up their class schedule, and purchase the requisite materials. If required textbooks are provided at no additional cost, the students may have the books handed to them on the first day of class. How then do you facilitate this process for Web-based distance students?

Certainly, with the advent of commercial online book distributors (e.g. Barnes & Noble and Amazon), some capability for book purchase without going to the campus exists (and likely at lower cost than the campus bookstore). However, textbooks are not always readily available from these sites and, if they are available, their low sales volume means delivery may take a great deal of time. Thus the campus bookstore must also be integrated into your services to Web-based students. If you are providing textbooks as a part of tuition, then you need to have a service for delivering the textbooks to the students' homes or offices.

Ideally, for purchasing books and materials, students would have access to the campus bookstore's product catalog. They would easily be able to look up the required books by entering a class name or number, automatically order the books over the Web, give their payment information, and have the books immediately mailed to them at their home.

For many campuses the ideal Web-based bookstore relationship is far from reality. Frequently, campus bookstores are not a part of the university; rather, they are contractors whose ability or desire to provide a Web-based interface for distance students may not be as keen as your need. In that case, you must find another means of providing the service to your distance students. Several options exist, though none is as easy as working to integrate the bookstore into your services.

- Creation of a distance student purchasing department where personnel take the orders and then do the footwork to purchase books and charge to the department. The department then bills and/or accepts payment directly from the student.
- Assign clerical personnel in each academic department to purchase and distribute specific textbooks based on need.
- Increase tuition by some amount to include all required textbooks. Textbooks are then purchased with the increased tuition and mailed by the bookstore after mass purchases are completed.
- Don't use textbooks. (Not recommended.) Instead provide all information via the Web.

In addition to textbooks, there are many other materials campus bookstores often make available (e.g. essay books, educational software, lab items, pencils and pens, test papers, article copies, etc.). Each of these may be an important part of the students' learning process as well as the only place students may access this equipment. The complexity of delivery of these items makes it very important to negotiate early and effectively to set up a system for distributing textbooks and materials to distance students.

Interesting bookstore link pages include:

- University of Utah Bookstore http://as400.utah.edu/cgi-db2/start.mac/start
- Brown University Bookstore http://bookstore.brown.edu/
- University of Maine http://www.umabookstore.com/

Marketing

If your institution is beginning to offer Web-based courses, or you are planning a strategic move to offer many more Web-based courses or entire degree programs, it is important that you obtain good marketing support. It is not uncommon that a university invests heavily in training faculty and in acquiring or creating Web-based courses, only to be disappointed when few students sign up for the courses. A concerted effort must be made to market the courses both through traditional means and via the Internet. Remember, because your students will be Internet-based, it is most likely that they will research their Web-based opportunities via the Internet.

Your best Internet marketing efforts are to provide an easy link from your institution's primary Web page. Also, be sure to provide the information to each of the major Web search engines (e.g. Yahoo, Altavista, Go, Excite, etc.). Select keyword registration that is likely to be used, such as "distance learning," "distance education," "online education," and "online degree." Finally, search out sites that are interested in providing lists of institutions with online courses. A few free common listings are given below.

- Virtual University Gazette http://www.geteducated.com/
- Cisco Educational Archives http://www.ibiblio.org/cisco/

- Schools on the Web (K-12) http://www.tenet.edu/education/main.html
- Education Network Australia http://www.edna.edu.au/EdNA

In addition to your Internet marketing efforts, traditional methods are still necessary to reach your community constituency with the news of your new offerings. Non-Internet marketing efforts that have worked with other institutions include:

- Radio advertisements placed during the morning and evening high traffic hours when workers are commuting.
- Brochures distributed via career magazines and newsletters.
- Advertisements in books that cater to Web-based learners, such as Petersons http://www.petersons.com/
- Newspaper advertising in your local community.
- Inserts and advertising with any normal mailings you do (e.g. course catalogs).

Alumni associations

The final area of Web-based support often overlooked is providing service to alumni. Many colleges are now using the Internet to offer graduates online classes, mentoring opportunities, and lifetime opportunities for career placement. All these activities fall under the rubric of "university advancement." Alumni services such as lifelong personal e-mail accounts, home pages for each graduating class and for regional alumni, and newsgroups on the Internet make it easier than ever for former students to keep in touch and for college fund raisers to find them.

Certainly, once you have graduated a number of students in Web-based courses you will have Internet-based alumni to serve. Just as these non-traditional students were not physically present on campus during their studies, they are unlikely to be able to come to campus as alumni. However, they are still an excellent resource for advertising, campus input, fund raising, and to serve as an example to future Web-based students. Providing online alumni services to traditional graduates can be beneficial as well. Many high schools, colleges, and universities lose track of their alumni within five years of graduation, leaving a rich resource of talent, networking, advice, and funding untapped. By providing a Web-based interface and some Web-based activities your institution can mine this group of former students.

Sometimes, universities will combine resources to access alumni. For example, in the United States, Yale, Stanford, and Princeton are collaborating to offer online courses to their alumni. Other universities may form alumni partnerships along lines of practice (e.g. medicine, nursing, education, social work) or along lines of matching needs in the community (e.g. library building, community involvement, regional development). Whatever the reason, keeping alumni involved in the university is important, and providing a Web presence is critical to a full offering of a Web-based support environment.

How should an alumni Web presence be built? What should be included? In this situation, it is best to look at good non-profit organizations and other excellent fund-raising sites – sites that have pull. The more visitors, the more opportunities the alumni association has to present options.

Let's look at some excellent "pull" sites in the non-profit arena that can inform us on how to build good alumni sites.

- http://www.amnesty.org. For those concerned about human rights, Amnesty International can relate exactly what is going on in practically every country in the world where abuses occur, and then describe what an individual can do about it.
- http://www.oncolink.org. For those concerned about cancer and who want to know about survival-rates and treatment options, OncoLink is a good site.
- http://metmuseum.org. Some sites can pull visitors because they are product-rich. The Metropolitan Museum, with its upscale online shop, is an example. Alumni sites that work in conjunction with gift shops or university bookstores can learn from this site.

Other sites pull visitors because they are service-rich, enabling the visitor to accomplish a task online. A good example would be a digital library site, or any college Web site that allows prospective students the opportunity to apply online.

Another visitor attraction is entertainment. Some nonprofit sites include games, unique movie footage, contests, music, and online exhibitions. An example of an "entertainment" draw would be the Metropolitan Museum's site on its reopened Greek Galleries. This site offers a "preview" of eighteen objects, views of the galleries, a timeline "illustrated with signal works of art," a map of the Mediterranean, and more. It is so alluring and so well done that many people spend hours there [http://www.metmuseum.org/htmlfile/newexhib/greek/greekl.htm]. This same type of offering can be used on your alumni site to identify who has been feted lately and who has published an important work, and to highlight student art or community accolades.

Good design and clever strategy are key to keeping alumni coming back and visiting your site. Consider the Metropolitan Museum's bottom menu bar, which constantly offers the following options:

- Membership
- Calendar
- Collections
- Exhibitions
- Information
- News
- Education
- Store
- Home

The most important pull strategy is involvement. If an organization can involve its visitors and entice them to come back again and again, then the site is operating at a new and effective level. Simply put, supporters will be able to move from visitor, to participant, to member of your community. A loyal member of your alumni community is the highest type of prospect.

Online education is one example of involvement. People who take an online course will visit that site repeatedly. They will be asking questions, viewing resources, downloading class material, consulting with the teacher one-to-one, and engaging their fellow classmates in meaningful chat. Well organized and well staffed online courses are perhaps the most powerful devices for "engaging" your members and friends.

Other examples of involvement include offering periodic chat sessions with "stars" or experts, online book clubs, online chat groups, online threaded discussion groups, and online "members only" interactive groups. Princeton University offers interactive areas for its alumni in each class. Princeton also hosts online exchanges on broad topics in which any alumni can participate. Examples include discussions on real estate and biomedical issues http://tigernet.princeton.edu/. If you would like to see an example of an "open" alumni exchange, see the one at Colby College, http://www.colby.edu/alumni/bulletin/index.html.

To summarize: mining alumni and keeping them loyal is of great benefit to Web-based education efforts. Alumni become future students, spread the word of your course offerings, and provide funding for future endeavors. Your alumni sites should offer something that will pull visitors not just once but repeatedly. Web designers should be creative, test ideas, and allow themselves to be surprised. Consider the unique information you want to present that might interest your potential constituents and build the site around it.

4 Developing faculty: the changed role of online instructors

Faculty development is critical to the success of any Web-based education effort. In fact, designing, creating, and implementing effective in-service training is the most efficient pathway to the long-term success of your Web-based distance education programs.

A key role change that faculty must begin to embrace in order to be effective in the online environment is that of facilitator or mentor. To use a theater analogy, the traditional instructor serves as the lead actor – the one who must carry the show, even though there is allowance for other characters to interact. In contrast, the online instructor is more like the director – one who ensures that all the characters play their part and that the show moves smoothly from beginning to end, adding his or her expertise only when the actors seem to need assistance. The director (teacher) leaves the content delivery to the script (Web pages and assignments) and the uniqueness of character development and nuances of meaning to the actors (the students).

A change from the traditional teaching role begins with faculty letting the technology become the information disseminator, while they rely on their mastery of the subject and their consummate skills in inducing students to discovery as the means to facilitate learning. The emphasis moves from presenting information to assisting students in identifying personal relevance and integrating it into their lives. Contrary to some beliefs, technology does not allow less knowledgeable instructors to become teachers. Rather, it requires the most knowledgeable instructors to participate. With the emphasis on individual guidance and problem-solving, it is required that the instructor be a master in the subject area and have a strong desire to assist students in the learning process.

Getting acceptance of this change in teaching paradigm and philosophy, as well as getting faculty involved and motivated toward the change, may be very difficult. In this information-flooded environment, teachers are already feeling the struggle of adapting to change; many feel they are barely staying afloat now. Teachers cope with changing student profiles, reduced resources, increased work loads, competition for research funds and enrollments, and verbalized expectations of service from a community to its educational agencies. When new learning technologies are added to the mix, these stressors can overload everyone concerned.

As if all this environmental change were not enough, teachers are also overwhelmed with the options for staff development and teaching skill development now available in printed form, conferences, and electronically on the Web. Already publishers produce numerous books of advice about faculty development and change management – as do a number of professional associations and other groups. This overload of information and opportunity can be readily found in numerous Internet sites. A listing of a few of these is below.

* *United Kingdom*
  Staff and Educational Development Association (SEDA) Environments http://www.seda.demon.co.uk/
  Networked Lifelong Learning http://www.shef.ac.uk/uni/projects/csnl/nll.html
  Innovations in Education and Teaching International Journal http://www.journals.tandf.co.uk/journals/routledge/14703297.html
* *Canada*
  Society for Teaching and Learning in Higher Education http://www.umanitoba.ca/academic_support/uts/stlhe
  NAWEB international conference for Web-based teaching and learning http://www.unb.ca/wwwdev/
  Office of Learning Technologies (Federal Government) http://olt-bta.hrdcdrhc.gc.ca
* *Australia*
  Higher Education Research and Development Society of Australasia (HERDSA) http://www.herdsa.org.au
  University of New England Style Guide of Online Teaching Materials http://www.une.au/online-info/style/
* *United States*
  Educause publications http://www.educause.edu
  American Association of Higher Education http://www.aahe.org
  Teaching Learning and Technology Group http://www.tltgroup.org

Designing a faculty development plan that will help teachers synthesize new knowledge and tailor the new technology and teaching strategies to their class needs is certainly a challenge. You must begin with some concept of how to approach the problem. Will your training be remedial or transformative, voluntary or mandated? How will you overcome some of the fear and resistance faculty will display? Will you provide this development opportunity through a professional development center, online or in a classroom, for credit or non-credit? Will you offer a smorgasbord of workshops and just-in-time assistance for teachers, or will you design a single all-encompassing development effort? Finally, what institutional strategic initiatives are reflected in the training you offer? All of these decisions will impact the acceptance of your development efforts.

Difficult transitions from classroom teaching to online facilitation

The teaching and learning environment in a traditional classroom is perceived as vastly different from that in the online environment. An issue that is frequently brought to the fore by faculty is that of visual cues on which they rely in the classroom and have no ability to use in the online environment. This lack of visual cueing becomes a rallying point for resistance and fear of transitioning to online classrooms.

In a traditional classroom, teachers rely on a number of visual and unobtrusive cues from their students. A quick glance, for example, reveals those who are attentively taking notes, pondering difficult concepts, or enthusiastically preparing to respond to the teacher's questions. The same glance uncovers those who are tense, frustrated, confused, tired, or bored. Teachers may rely on walking around the room and evaluating the number of highlighted passages in a textbook, the pages of notes a student may take, or the doodling a student may be doing to pass the time. The effective teacher consciously and subconsciously analyzes these visual cues with great subtlety and clarity. As a result, the delivery of information – and often the course content itself – is adapted to meet the unique mix of student moods, characteristics, and needs at any one time. To these teachers, having an instinctive feel for their students is just "good teaching."

However, as Willis (1998) indicated, "while natural instinct may help, it is the dynamics at play in and around the traditional classroom setting that increases teacher effectiveness." Teachers often fail to realize that many interaction opportunities actually occur *outside* of class during spontaneous discussions between students or between a student and the teacher. Students also continue their learning while meeting informally on a homework assignment or over lunch while discussing mutual interests that may relate to the class topics. Learning more often takes place during these spontaneous communication sessions than during the lecture portion of instruction.

Facilitators and mentors

Teachers may lack confidence in the new role they are expected to play, and may be fearful of failing to teach well. Because of the key role of technology as the link between teacher and students, it is important that faculty gain comfort and proficiency in using electronic communications (e-mail, discussion boards, chat, whiteboards). This requires a practical understanding of each technology's strengths and weaknesses, as well as strategies for their use. Providing instruction on these technologies is essential, as is providing opportunities for practice prior to implementation of a course. The best way to provide this type of instruction and practice is via a faculty development course that is taught online. It is only by actually experiencing the online environment as a student that teachers finally understand student fears, stress, frustrations, and joys in learning in the Web-based environment.

In order to be an effective mentor online, the teacher must also appreciate their students' lifestyles. That students live in different communities, geographic regions, and especially in other countries, challenges the instructor to find a common community link or reference point. It is probable that many students' life experiences, living conditions, and culture will be foreign to the faculty member as well as to other class participants. In order to form some type of common community, it is up to the instructor to create an environment in which discussion of similarities and differences is brought up early in the class and capitalized upon in discussions throughout the term. One way to do this is through introductions early in the course via discussion board postings. These introductions can then be followed up with links to student pictures, Web pages, and geographic or cultural information. For example, one instructor would begin each course with a map of North America and Europe – from which the student base for the class was drawn – and then place a picture of each student with an arrow pointing to the student's geographic location. The student's picture was hotlinked to the student's Web page that described his or her background and interests. This graphical and textual system provided a foundation for both the instructor and other students to "see" each other and to begin to form their own community of learning and to find a common reference point.

Another important method of evaluating the lifestyle of Web-based students is to look at the profile of your class. Traditionally, in the United States, distance students have been older (average ages 30–50), have families, and work in part or full-time jobs while pursuing their education. This means they have very busy lives and many commitments that strive for equal attention with learning. These students elect to learn via online courses because it suits their schedule and allows them to fit learning into nontraditional times. It is important to understand your students' time frames for learning and particularly for interaction with you. It is up to you to cater to this lifestyle as much as possible in planning communication activities in your course. For example, even if you hold regular office hours from 9.00 a.m. to 10.00 a.m. on Tuesdays, it is likely that many of your students will not be available to ask questions at that time. Instead, you need to offer your chat office hours at typical nonworking times like 9.00 p.m. on Thursday evening or 10.00 a.m. on Saturday morning. In doing this, you show respect for your students and demonstrate an understanding of their unique challenges. The same rule would work for any synchronous activities you may plan for your course. One well respected instructor always required one or two synchronous activities during the term. In a class of twenty to twenty-five students, she would schedule these synchronous activities (e.g. a simulation performed via chat) by offering three alternative times and asking class members to sign up for the times that best suited their schedule. Typical time selections might be Tuesday at noon, Wednesday at 9.00 p.m., and Saturday at 8.00 a.m. Providing both day and evening times as well as a weekend time would net full participation because students would likely find one that could mesh with their schedule.

Fostering a sense of community

Almost a decade ago, Moore (1992) found that transactional distance could be a definite challenge in distance education. The question then becomes: what is the best way to create a virtual community from a group of individuals separated by time and space? This is important not only from a student's perspective, but also from the teacher's perspective. Many faculty state that one of the benefits of teaching is that sense of community and self-worth they derive from working with students in the classroom – from seeing "the light bulb go on" – and *knowing* that their assistance was key to the learning. The challenge is to create this same feeling, this social presence, in the online environment. In order to do that, some means of helping both students and teachers to become comfortable expressing their feelings in writing is key to this success. The process would begin with the instructor modeling the inclusion of feelings in anything written. For example, in the welcome to the course letter, the instructor might express *excitement* for the course beginning, *concern* about potential problems, and provide some self-disclosure about his or her own *fears* and challenges with the online learning process that might match the students' concerns.

When students were asked to advise faculty concerning the instructor's role in distance instruction, Hiltz (1994) found that responsiveness, online communication competence, and organization were the key factors for success that students cited. Specifically, teachers were urged to be flexible in their presentations and activities, to provide frequent and directed questions and responses, to acknowledge comments made by students, to encourage "lurkers" to contribute to the group, and to provide periodic updates and reviews of discussions. In short, it seems that students desire direction and reinforcement, but not an iron hand.

Fostering community is both challenging and rewarding in the Web-based environment. When it is done well, students report that they actually learned more, felt closer to their peers, and got to know their instructor better than they ever did in the traditional classroom. Also, when an instructor experiences success in fostering community, he or she frequently testifies that students' responses to discussion postings were more thoughtful, the essays seemed to be better written, and the instructor felt as if he or she better understood each individual student's abilities compared with their traditional students studying the same subject. It is likely that these feelings of connection, in spite of the lack of visual cues and physicality, are realistic because of the one-on-one mentoring relationship that develops in any learning community – but is particularly encouraged in an online community where the instructor has taken extra care to foster it.

Transformative communication

In the past, traditional learning tended to be didactic, following the transmission model of instruction. The instructor – as the master of the topic – transmits knowledge to the students. The student then somehow processes the information and proves his or her knowledge by regurgitation in essay form or in some type of written or oral final exam. The difficulty with this model is that each student learns differently and there is no good way to measure the depth of knowledge or the transformation the student may have undergone during the learning process – a transformation that may lead to significant innovation in the future. Furthermore, the transmission model relies on passive learning with little to no socialization. People, however, are social, perceptual creatures whose preferred mode of learning is experiential. People often need to work in small groups, to share their knowledge, and to collaborate on complex tasks. Finally, people learn best and retain knowledge best when their learning is perceived as practical, situated, and directly applicable to their current lives. This is true of children and adults alike.

Pea (1994) describes a transformative view of communication between teacher and student as a generative process: Instructors learn along with their students. As a result, instructors and students alike are transformed as learners by the process of communication. Through such discourse within the learning community, the active learning that occurs can begin to push the frontiers of knowledge and generate further innovation.

Instructors assist in activating this transformative process by providing distinct tasks that help students generalize their mental models to new contexts. The teacher's role then becomes one of modeling and allowing constructive discourse and negotiating meaning among the students – a role that not only provides for the transmission of information but actually builds knowledge and innovation through the social support of the efforts of the learning community as a whole. The key – and often most frightening aspect – to this change in instructor behavior is to give up control over the learning process. It requires the teacher to trust that students can and will learn without the instructor being the sole communicator of knowledge. In the transformation model, students and instructor alike no longer draw only on classroom resources; they now access a number of people, activities, and knowledge databases through the Internet.

Sherry and Wilson (1997) articulated several key indicators that transformative communication is happening and that the learner support environment is effective. These indicators are captured in Table 4.1.

Through collaborative activities and experiences, the class group becomes cohesive and develops into a dynamic learning community. The question each instructor must answer is "How can I create or model an environment that encourages learners to take responsibility for their own learning?" To start, the teacher must shift focus from teaching to support. As in the discussion above on changing from a disseminator of information to a facilitator of learning, in transformative communication the instructor becomes the mentor by offering support and guidance based on his or her years of experience and knowledge of the topic.

Wilson and Ryder (1998) outlined seven ways in which an instructor can create a common pattern of mutually supportive interaction in the class:

- Encourage students to articulate their learning needs.
- Provide a public forum that promotes group contributions and assistance.
- Engage in help consultation, both between the learner and the teacher and among student peers.
- Assess learning through a combination of self-assessment and consensual agreement.
- Share difficult solutions with the entire class – perhaps through a restatement of the original problem and its solution.
- Archive interactions and solutions for future reference.
- Repeat this process, or any part, if necessary to support learning.

Table 4.1 Indicators of transformative communication

Transformative communication	Effective learner support
Students teach the instructor something new.	Students solve their own problems and share their solutions with others.
Student goes beyond the textbook or instructor note pages to reveal differences of opinion among the experts.	Students make presentations to classmates, announcing the finding of a solution to a common problem.
More emphasis is placed on finding support for a position than on conforming to authority.	Solutions to common problems are codified and shared with succeeding groups.
Students participate in setting the agenda for class and help to choose content or learning methods, or both.	Effective learning resources are found, "stolen," or developed, and are made available to the entire learning community.
Students are calling the instructor's attention to valuable learning resources.	Students are encouraged and rewarded for taking initiative.
Students are having conversations with knowledgeable people the instructor doesn't know.	Students are made to feel that their unique strengths are valued, and that they have something to offer the larger learning community.
While the instructor establishes expectations and sets clear assessment standards, the students collaboratively guide much of their own learning.	The informal culture encourages risk-taking and innovation, and inclusion of diverse needs.
The instructor finds himself or herself saving student work – not merely as examples, but as content resources for future reference.	The cultural values of learner support are reflected in the formal rules and reward structure of the organization.

Long before textbooks, instruction began as an oral tradition. It truly was based in oratory – the "sage on the stage." With widespread literacy, the "sage" role began to be shared with experts who wrote textbooks. But those textbooks still needed some interpretation by teachers. In the age of technology and programmed instruction, instructional designers (teachers) thought they were in the business of designing lessons to meet specific learning objectives. But then the constructivist movement – and now communications technologies themselves – seem to be threatening this concept as the sole way to support learning. Increasingly, some researchers assert that the majority of learning, in fact, takes place outside the school environment. Whatever the truth may be, it is important to reassess the instructor role. It is important to determine what the support of learning actually entails and how that transforms the teaching relationship to more non-instructional forms of learning.

The love–hate relationship of faculty with online instruction

Throughout this chapter, we have been reviewing the changing role of instructors in the online environment. Indeed, this role is also changing in the traditional classroom environment. Interestingly, the reasons faculty state for dislike of online instruction are frequently the same reasons other faculty cite for their love of online instruction. (Table 4.2.)

Table 4.2 Faculty reasons for their feelings about online instruction

Reason	Love	Hate
The use of technology	I find that technology is exciting and it frees the student and teacher to expand their horizons outside of the instructor's knowledge base during the course.	I find that technology is frustrating, frightening, or takes too much time. It also removes control of the learning from the teacher.
The absence of visual cues	I recognize that I may not be good at reading visual cues. Written words and evaluation of student knowledge provides much more information for adapting the learning environment.	I need the physical contact with students in order to solidify emphasis and to "see" the students learning. I am rewarded by "seeing" the light bulb go off as the student grasps meaning.
The need to work during non-traditional hours	I enjoy the freedom of not being on campus all the time. It is nice to connect with students at times when they are available and actively pursuing my input. I can adapt my personal life around varied hours.	I already have too much to do and need to have consistent, specific hours in order to have a life outside of teaching. I cannot adapt my personal life around varied hours.
The change in the role of the teacher from knowledge disseminator to facilitator or mentor	I am confident in my knowledge and my ability to work with students and guide their learning. I am equally rewarded by learning along with them.	I am confident in my knowledge and confident that I know what is the best way for the student to learn this topic. Allowing students more freedom in how to structure learning only adds to the myriad of guidance requests I already need to serve.

Faculty development issues

By any measure, the goal of faculty development is change. However, change in complex educational environments is difficult to accept, let alone promote. An additional challenge is the technical and administrative infrastructure in place at many institutions. This infrastructure may (unintentionally) act as a barrier to change, while at the same time demanding that faculty not only make changes to the online environment, but make them very quickly. Educational institutions are often static bureaucracies lacking dynamic flexibility. As a result, emphasis is placed on changing students, staff, and faculty instead of changing the institution itself.

The rigid departmental structure of many institutions encourages low faculty interdependence and creates an environment where faculty face a plethora of contrasting goals and expectations. The strategic goals of a Web-based distance program, for example, may be in conflict with the goals for departmental development. Finally, institutions that reward faculty for research and publication (tenure) often end up unknowingly providing a disincentive to participation in distance education. The reality is that developing Web-based courses, undertaking changes in faculty roles, and encouraging students to take responsibility for their own learning is not easy or comfortable. Institutions need to take stock of their strategic goals, align them with departments and provide good incentive for faculty participation. Without those steps, it is likely that only early adopters or faculty without loyalty to the institution will put in the time and energy necessary to move education into the online learning environment.

Promotion and tenure. Administrators and tenure committees must carefully assess how to include Web-based development and instruction efforts in their evaluations. For example, traditional methods of garnering student feedback on teachers or of sitting in a class to watch a faculty member teach do not work in the Web-based environment. Supervisors and committee members need to develop new tools for evaluating instruction in the online community. They may wish to assess the instructional impact and effectiveness of courses through Web-based instruments students are instructed to complete. They may need to determine other ways to measure teacher success (e.g. read instructor postings to class discussion boards, evaluate interactions in chat rooms, interview online students by phone regarding their observations of the course).

Publishing. Publishing traditionally focuses on the development, review, and distribution of printed material through refereed journals in the instructor's field of expertise. Acceptance and encouragement of publishing outside the instructor's field is needed to encourage quality teaching and research in the Web-based environment. Most online education publications are made through educational journals, though a few other fields are now incorporating articles regarding online teaching (e.g. nursing and computer science).

Release time or overload pay. Adapting traditional instruction to online delivery demands concerted and time-consuming effort. Expecting faculty to develop and deliver a quality course in addition to their regular teaching/research load is not reasonable. Progressive institutions typically provide release time at least on a one-to-one basis – release from teaching one four-credit-hour class for developing one online four-credit-hour class. Alternatively, some institutions offer overload pay at the same rate as teaching an equivalent credit-hour course. Some institutions also grant release time for professional development in the field of online education, and for internships in online classes. In the case of the internship, an instructor is granted release time from one class while co-teaching an online class with an experienced instructor.

Course load. It is important to address the issue of work load proactively. Research is still meager on course load comparisons. Several practitioners report that teaching a class of more than twenty students online is too time-consuming. Others report that teaching forty to fifty students is their limit. Undoubtedly, the difficulty lies in judging the interactivity of the course and the required interactivity of the instructor. The question also arises in how to compare face-to-face class numbers with online numbers. The key in determining course load is to realize that in a quality online environment, the instructor is performing much more as a one-on-one mentor for the student than in the traditional classroom. When taking that into consideration, many institutions have set online class sizes at similar levels to graduate instruction (twelve to fifteen students per class).

Faculty mentoring

Faculty mentoring helps to address the lack of confidence teachers may be reluctant to share. It is easy to feel alone when teaching a Web-based course. This is particularly true when teaching for the first time, and almost always true for adjunct instructors who may not have any regular relationship with the campus. One strategy for addressing this problem is through the development of a virtual faculty mentoring and support network that serves the same function as your campus-based teaching and learning centers. These networks can be formal or informal, depending on the needs of the instructors. The key is to get administration commitment for participation and to have specific personnel assigned to monitor the network, answer questions, and provide assistance on a daily basis. A second vital part of faculty mentoring is to match an experienced online instructor with someone who is new to the environment. The veteran instructor then becomes the primary personal support for the new instructor. Once initiated, mentoring programs take on a life of their own. With the proper care and nurturing at the onset, such programs can prove invaluable to the entire faculty community – both traditional and online – at your institution.

Online teacher communities

One of the first requests from faculty during their transition to online learning is to access research, best practice examples, and a variety of other resources that they can review and evaluate on their own. A number of list-serves and other types of Web-based communities exist to support online teaching. These virtual communities provide a place for members to exchange ideas, troubleshoot problems, and share research and other information. Subscribing to two or three of these communities would be a first step in teacher support. You might suggest that instructors subscribe individually, or, if staff feel overwhelmed by all the information, you may even want to assign a faculty developer to subscribe to multiple Web-based communities and then review and select pertinent information that meets the needs of his or her faculty contingency. A brief list and description of some of the well established support communities is below.

- *Distance Education Online Symposium (DEOS)* http://www.cde.psu.edu/ ACSDE/DEOS.html This extensive networking site was established in 1991 by the American Center for the Study of Distance Education at Pennsylvania State University. The symposium comprises DEOSNEWS, an electronic journal for practitioners and managers, and DEOS-L, an electronic forum. The purpose of DEOS is to disseminate information and to support international computer conferencing through systems accessible to professionals and students in the field of distance and technology-mediated education. DEOSNEWS publishes articles on topics such as distance education theory, the use of audio and video communications, course design and development, and adult education. It is accessed by over 4,000 subscribers in sixty-eight countries. DEOS-L, the interactive list-serve component of DEOS, has over 1,500 subscribers who participate in online discussions in the areas of research, current issues and professional networking.
- *National Grid for Learning (NGFL)* http://www.ngfl.gov.uk/ The NGFL initiative in the United Kingdom marks the most sustained and extensive commitment to educational information and communications technology by any government to date. The objectives of the NGFL include ensuring all of the 30,000 UK schools have access to the Internet by 2002, training over 500,000 teachers in new technologies, developing an interconnected network of services for teachers, and providing a variety of professional support through Virtual Teacher Centers.
- *International Center for Distance Learning (ICDL), Open University* http://www-icdl.open.ac.uk/ An international center for research, teaching, consultancy, information and publishing activities based in the Institute of Educational Technology. ICDL promotes international research and collaboration by providing information from its library and databases; other audiences are reached through publications. An essential knowledge resource built up over fifteen years is its distance education library and databases. ICDL distance education databases contain information on over 31,000 distance learning programs and courses, mostly in the Commonwealth countries, over 1,000 institutions teaching at a distance worldwide, and over 12,000 abstracts of books, journal articles, research reports, conference papers, dissertations and other types of literature relating to all aspects of the theory and practice of distance education.
- *Global Distance Education Net by the World Bank* http://www1.worldbank. org/ disted/ A knowledge guide to distance education designed to help clients of the World Bank and others interested in using distance education for human development. The Network consists of a core site located at the World Bank and regional sites in all parts of the world. Topics include teaching and learning online, technology descriptions, distance education management, and maintenance of policies and programs

- *Dissemination of Open and Distance Learning (DODL)* http://www.idb. hist.no/ DoODL/ DODL is a project granted within the European Commission program SOCRATES, with eight partners in five different European countries: Finland, Greece, the Netherlands, Norway and the United Kingdom. The objectives of the group include defining models for collaboration between European academic institutions, enhancing the skills of teachers, trainers and managers, and investigating tools to organize and enhance the online learning environment.
- *Commonwealth of Learning* http://www.col.org/ An intergovernmental organization created by Commonwealth heads of government to encourage the development and sharing of distance education knowledge, resources and technologies. The site contains a variety of resources around collaboration, training, and capacity building.
- *American Distance Education Consortium (ADEC)* http://www.adec.edu/ An American consortium of about 50 universities and colleges providing distance education programs and services, with particular emphasis on electronic delivery. The site includes information on the many courses available online from participating institutions. It also includes papers on distance teaching technologies, bibliographies, courseware tools and other online resources, discussion papers, news on policy debates and new developments, and links to international bodies. The site is frequently updated.
- *Athabasca University Resources in Distance Education (RIDE)* http://ccism. pc.athabascau.ca/html/ccism/deresrce/de.htm Athabasca University is a leading Canadian provider of open and distance learning. RIDE is a very comprehensive resource of distance education information and best practices. Sections include: Internet education – guides to searching the Internet, online courses, navigation tools, relevant list-serves and usenet groups (and links with the major ones); Searching the Web – search engines, virtual libraries, subject indices, databases, selected catalogs of online journals and magazines; Distance education and Web design; Educational technology resources – delivery systems, theories of learning, and issues such as quality, copyright, and social factors in learning.
- *Distance Education Clearinghouse* http://www.uwex.edu/disted/home.html A treasure house of comprehensive up-to-date and archival material on all aspects of distance and flexible learning and technology-mediated education. The Distance Education Clearinghouse is managed by the university of Wisconsin-Extension, and includes information from that University plus national and international sources. It is easy to navigate through the many sections and material is added regularly. Areas of particular interest include technology and network options, the design of effective technology-mediated programs, online courses offered, a database of conferences of interest to distance educators, policy and (American) legislative news, and a range of papers, bibliographies, and links with sites around the world.
- *Education Network Australia (EdNA)* Established in 1995 by Australia's federal and state Ministers of Education and Training as a national electronic

network to facilitate cooperation among all education sectors. The site provides a directory of online education and training information and services as a "one-stop shop" of Australian resources and material useful for education and training.

- *TECFA Education and Technologies* http://tecfa.unige.ch/ TECFA (Technologies de formation et apprentissage) is an academic unit of the University of Geneva with teaching and research interests in educational technology. The research section of the site includes material on collaborative projects of traditional and distance universities in Europe on the use of technology-mediated education to increase real and virtual mobility of students. The Virtual Library is an easy-to-use database of material under four broad themes of educational technology, educational software, learning environments, and technologies for distance education. There is a wealth of material on computer-mediated communications, virtual reality, and applications such as MUDs and MOOs.

There can be no denying that the ultimate success or failure of your Web-based program is tied to the enthusiasm and support of your faculty. Administrators and teachers alike should actively identify and resolve faculty development issues early and provide a continuing network of information, training, support, and sharing.

5 Designing courses and curriculum

Before beginning to design an online course or a curriculum containing several courses, it is important for you to first define online instruction for your specific course(s). Not every online course is taught 100 percent on the Web. In fact, the majority of online courses are hybrids of traditional classroom environments, interactive video environments, and even correspondence courses. Forms of online instruction include:

- Sharing information on a Web site (examples: course syllabus, instructor notes, test results).
- Providing practice for new concepts by using an online tool such as a simulation or game.
- Conducting asynchronous discussions by using a threaded discussion tool (e.g. WebBoard or a CMS discussion board).
- Conducting synchronous discussions using chat software.
- Communicating one-to-one or one-to-many via e-mail for instructional purposes.
- Holding office hours via chat.
- Giving practice tests or self-evaluations by using online forms and databases.
- Submitting assignments electronically via e-mail attachments, discussion board postings, and chat transcripts.
- Delivering library resources via the Internet through electronic databases or electronic books/papers on reserve.

Your course may use all of these forms of instruction or only a few, depending on the needs of your environment. A course taught exclusively online would best use all of these forms of communication and teaching in order to ensure that student participation and understanding are maximized.

Before beginning to think about the technology and your online course, it is wise to review other courses of similar topic and scope that are already available online. By doing this you will get ideas about how the technology was used and you will be able to evaluate what translates to your environment. Also, your evaluation of the effectiveness of the courses will help you to determine what you like or don't like. Developing an online course should not be done in a vacuum. The technology is too complex and the opportunity for innovation too great to leave it to a solitary endeavor of trial and error. Two excellent resources provide examples of online courses in a variety of topics.

*   World Lecture Hall http://www.utexas.edu/world/lecture/
*   University of Arkansas http://waltoncollege.uark.edu/disted/decnew2/online_ course_examples.htm

If you don't find your course topic covered in these resources, begin searching the net for online courses in your area and contact the teachers or institutions to request access for review. You may be surprised at how much most institutions are willing to share their expertise. Be sure to jot down ideas that will help with your course development and questions you may want to ask the instructor or others in your field regarding the delivery of information and selection of activities.

When you have completed your review of existing Web-based courses in your area of interest, it is time to take those first steps toward designing your own curriculum and courses. Step one is to follow the rules of basic logic and organization you probably learned in your writing composition courses – that is, to make an outline. This is a fairly easy step, yet one of the most important, and frequently overlooked by new course designers. It can save you a lot of work down the road. Your outline needs to illustrate all of the important elements of your curriculum or course and how they interrelate. It is not necessary to make this outline a formal structure; however, you should group major components of your course together in order to see what distinct learning units may begin to emerge. Once you have created the outline, you should then draw lines between the elements to indicate how they are linked together. These lines will help dictate your course organization, navigation, and hyperlinks.

If you are visually oriented, you may prefer to begin your outlining process with the use of mind maps or structure maps. These are graphical representations of all the elements of your topic and their relationships. Figure 5.1 is an example mind map that was constructed for this book. The picture was developed using a software tool called Inspiration™. Note that the central cloud represents the book as a whole. Radiating from that central theme are the major components of the book (which became chapters), and branching from each component are subtopics. Your course or an entire curriculum offering can be mapped in a similar fashion. Pay special attention to the linking arrows. These arrows represent the interrelationship of subtopics both within a major component, as well as across components. In the example below, the component of support systems has direct relationships to the components of faculty development, course design, planning, and miscellaneous issues.

Though only the major components are illustrated in Figure 5.1, you may wish to build separate mind maps for each learning unit of your course. On a curriculum level, you certainly want to illustrate the relationships between courses. These relationships are what ultimately provide the opportunities for linking, remediation, and advanced knowledge development within your course or curriculum. It also

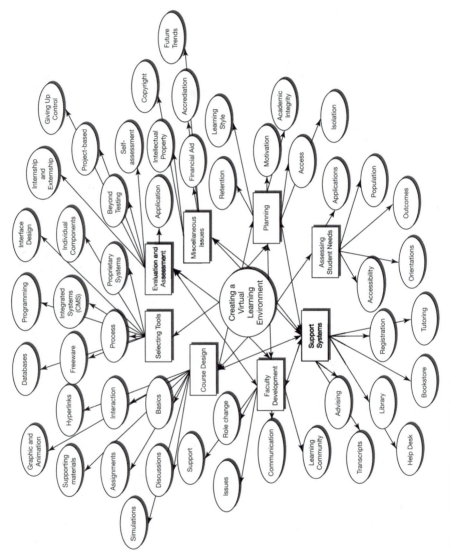

Figure 5.1 Mind map of this book

provides information about discrete elements that may be shared across units or courses, and thus influence your design structure. You may choose to use the mind map and its depiction of relationships to dictate a different organizational structure for your course or at least to provide alternative paths to knowledge. Finally, these linkages help you to determine where and how to articulate and reinforce relationships within a course and within specific topics or subtopics.

Using a graphical representation of an outline does not meet everyone's needs. Remember, this is just one way of delineating a course structure. You need to create a way that best suits you and other teachers who may be sharing information and resources with you.

Web page design basics for the uninitiated

In a "perfect" world, the actual design and building of Web pages would be left to a team of designers with those specific skills. In a team environment, the instructor or content expert would provide the Web design expert with wordprocessed documents representing each distinct learning unit, a storyboard or prototype of suggested tables and graphics, and a description of interactions. This Web designer would then undertake the design and Web implementation of all these materials, leaving the instructor to teach the course. Unfortunately, it is a rare institution that provides this type of Web designer support. All too often, the entire responsibility for Web page design is left to the instructor – hopefully, with support by some technical personnel or a Help Desk.

Whether you are fortunate enough to have a Web designer to do the work for you, or you have to develop the Web pages yourself, it is important for the instructor or course developer to have a good understanding of Web page design basics. Though you may be an excellent instructor and have an admirable structure and design for the delivery of your online course, without following good Web page design rules, your course will be weakened and may even become confusing to your students.

When you first think about design, it helps to identify the usual elements contained within a Web page.

- Formatted and colored text
- Still or moving images such as photographs, animations or video clips
- Links that provide navigation – they take you to another location in the same page or to another Web page
- Formatted tables
- Horizontal rule lines

The way you use each of the above page elements will determine the formality of your pages, as well as provide a structure or framework by which your students may come to a better understanding of the material. For example, colors can be used as visual cues of topical changes, glossary words, new information, or interactions.

Many of the questions to consider in designing individual Web pages are similar to the questions you will ask in designing the overall course. The difference here is that now you are evaluating discrete elements of your course and determining how many of them will go on a single Web page. Ask yourself the following questions for each page you design.

*   What's the purpose of the page? Is this an introductory page, an advanced page, a glossary entry, an assignment, fun links?
*   Who is your intended audience? Knowing your readers helps you shape the information content and pick a consistent voice to address them.
*   How do you intend to structure the information? It's common to see at least two levels of hierarchy: a top level index and second level pages. Put as much content toward the top of a hierarchy as possible. (This way, even the casual reader can quickly grasp the sort of information you're presenting.) The easiest way to lay out your information is by dividing it into major categories or concept chunks.
*   How will you break your topics into subtopics and what are their relationships? If you have several small topics, group them onto a single page.
*   How many links will you include and for what purpose? Remember, you can create links that are internal to the page as well as to pages outside of the specific page. Links may be used for general navigation, but also for context specific development – remediation, glossaries, further information.
*   How important is your navigation structure? With open linking, students can start to browse your Web page at any number of points, then navigate them in arbitrary fashion, choosing where to start and stop browsing. If you want to dictate sequencing, you need to plan your linking structure carefully.
*   How many pictures, sounds, and movies should you use and how will they be placed or linked? The fancier and more complex your pages are, the more work and time you'll need to develop them. While multimedia elements definitely add pizzazz to your pages, they also can make a page take too long to load, delaying the student from accessing the information they desire. Multimedia aspects should be used for specific and important instruction purposes, not just to add excitement to a page.

Web page design

There are several key elements you want to consider and specifically plan when building Web pages.

*   Designing the look and feel of your site
*   Creating storyboards and templates
*   Determining page length
*   Creating accessible/usable content
*   Using graphics that are meaningful
*   Selecting color and fonts that assist learning
*   Finishing touches

Designing the look and feel

Prior to learning the software of an HTML editor or building your Web page in your word processor, take some time to think about the "look and feel" of your Web site. Who do you want to see it? What impression do you want them to have of you after looking at it? Why should you choose certain colors or fonts? How do you make your site look consistent and professional? All of these are questions that are part of basic design philosophy. Spending at least half of your development time in planning your Web page will save you many hours in creating or redoing your Web pages later.

Creating storyboards and templates

A storyboard is a planning tool used by many graphic designers, video designers, and Web page designers. It is simply a set of drawings that show the intended layout of your project. For example, in this book you may have noticed elements that are repeated – the chapter title and a page number. A course Web page template provides the foundation for all pages within the course. The template might include a navigation graphic, the header graphic, and the size and style of content text on each page. Additionally, within the content section several decisions might be made for consistency (e.g. all text heads use a brown color; tables use a yellow background with brown text; the top head is a larger font size than the rest of the text.

These decisions are transmitted to everyone concerned by drawing up several storyboards first, then using a graphics program to develop a template for every page. An example of a template storyboard for a course is shown in Figure 5.2.

Note that when you begin with storyboards, they don't have to be perfect sketches. You want to concentrate on getting your design ideas down on paper, then you can perfect them in your graphics package (i.e. Photoshop, PaintShop Pro, Illustrator, etc.). A template consists of all those parts of the page that will remain constant. If you design a template first, you can then copy it for each subsequent page and save yourself a lot of time in making your Web site look professional.

Determining page length

People have many choices in setting up their screen displays. Sizes of 640×480 pixels or 800×600 or $1,024 \times 768$ are commonly used. As screen size increases, resolution options will also continue to change. Depending on reading needs and monitor size, settings may be changed to make the type larger or smaller at any time. This means you must design your pages so that the information is presented nicely in any of these formats. The rule of thumb is to design pages in short, clearly segmented chunks. Keep pages concise. If you want to present larger portions of information (like this chapter), then be sure to provide internal navigation links to those sections in order to prevent the reader from having to scroll through many pages of reading.

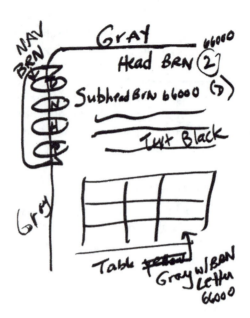

Figure 5.2 Example of a template storyboard for a course

A good rule of thumb for writing a page meant to be read onscreen is to make it no longer than two to three 640×480 screens' worth of information (this is the equivalent of two to three double-spaced typed screens in your word processor), including local navigational links at either the beginning or the end of the page layout. If you make the page longer than the window, the student has to remember too much information that has already scrolled off the screen.

Keep closely related information within the confines of a single Web page, particularly when you expect the user to print or save the text. If you want to provide a good online interface for pages and easy printing or saving of the content, divide the page into chunks of two to three printed pages of information, including inline graphics or figures. Or provide a link to a separate file that contains the full-length text combined into one page.

Creating accessible/usable content

While the graphic design of your pages should be pleasing, it is ultimately the content that determines a page's value to others. Use graphics and color and vary the font size to enhance your page, but make sure your page also works when viewed as straight text. Also, if your text is to be viewed in a frame, make sure it can be opened as a separate window as well, making it easier to view and print the page if desired.

Pare down your text. Reading a screen is not as easy as reading hard copy. Usability tests show that people will skip over text that they consider nonessential.

They don't like to scroll. Often students will scan a page reading only the text of the hypertext links before they choose their next destination.

Settle on as few heading styles and subtitles as are necessary to organize your content, then use your chosen styles consistently. Just because your Web page development tool provides six levels of headings doesn't mean that you should use them all in a single page. Use heading levels in order, with a level 1 heading at the top and, if necessary, several level 2 headings. Be aware that different Web browsers use different spacing and fonts. Use the heading levels to indicate structure, as they were intended.

Avoid overusing bold face, italics, and multiple font styles in your text. One thing you can do to ease the monotony and visual strain of reading lots of text on the computer screen is to use the Block Quote paragraph format and Unnumbered List format. Both formats result in indented text blocks that shorten lines of text, keep margins clear, and generally make the page easier to scan. You can also insert horizontal lines to visually separate sections of your document.

Graphics that are meaningful

Graphics add a lot to the visual appeal and information content of a page. But poor use of graphics can frustrate your students or keep them from understanding the message you're trying to send. Practically every published Web author will agree: keep images small! You should aim to keep the total file size of images used on a page to less than 50k. Remember that not everyone seeing your page has a high-speed connection. If you need to use a large image, you might want to consider using a thumbnail of the image and then linking it to the full-size copy. You can reduce file size by using design programs to eliminate unnecessary colors.

Use background graphics intelligently. Backgrounds that are "loud" make it extremely hard to read the text on top of them. Don't let your backgrounds interfere with the message you're sending the student. For a background to work well, color contrast is not enough. The background either needs to be very light (for dark text) or very dark (for light text). A background that contains an image should have low contrast, so it's not too distracting.

The two types of image formats used by most Web browsers are GIF (CompuServe Graphics Interchange Format, .GIF extension) and JPEG (Joint Photographic Experts Group, .JPG extension). The JPEG format works best for photos and continuous tone images. The GIF format works best for inline images, line art drawings, most logos, and screen captures. Both formats should use a resolution of 72 d.p.i. (dots per inch). You do not need more d.p.i. resolution, as most screens cannot provide a better resolution than 72 d.p.i. Keeping the resolution small also helps to keep the file sizes small so that they load faster.

Colors and fonts that assist learning

It is tempting to add lots of colors and font styles to a page just because you can. But the result is more likely to frustrate a student and detract from the message you're trying to get across. After all, it's the content you want your audience to focus on, and that means presenting a page that's easy to read. Even though most graphical browsers use a proportionally spaced font such as Times Roman as the default for text, many browsers are user-configurable, meaning the user can choose any font for viewing your pages.

Consider typography as the tool you, the artist, use to paint patterns on the page. The first thing your student sees is not the title or other details of the page, but the overall pattern and contrast of the page. The learner scans the page first as a purely graphic pattern, then he or she begins to track and decode type and page elements. Good typography depends on the visual contrast between one font and another and the contrast between text blocks and the surrounding empty space. There are a few basic typographic principles that can help make your pages easier on the eye:

- Avoid overusing bold face, italics, and multiple font styles in your text. Too much contrast is just as bad as no contrast at all.
- Making text uniformly bigger doesn't help at all, and only contributes to making the pages longer.
- Boldface fonts become monotonous very quickly, because if everything is bold, nothing stands out, and it looks like you're shouting at your students. Using all upper case can have the same jarring effect.
- Choose a few heading styles to organize your content, and then use your chosen styles consistently. Regular, repeated patterns help learners quickly establish the location and organization of your information, and increase the overall legibility of your pages.
- Use white space judiciously. Don't put blank lines or horizontal rules everywhere or your pages will look choppy. (Plus, you're trying to keep page length to a minimum.)
- Thoughtful and consistent use of color in backgrounds can really help pull your pages together into a cohesive presentation. In general, light pastel backgrounds are best for reading substantial amounts of text. If you are showing a lot of pictures, a black background can make your photos look good and give your pages a gallery-like effect. Using tiled backgrounds makes everything above them "float," causing your readers to work much harder to read your text. Using a white background can make text look good and your document look clean, but if you have a lot of pages, it can be extremely wearing on the eyes.

Finishing touches

Last, but not least, are the finishing elements that are considered the hallmarks of the work of a professional Web author: headers, footers, contact information, navigation, links, and time stamps.

- *Headers.* A consistent title design at the top of your Web page allows your students to immediately know what the main point of the document is, and what (if any) relationship the page may have to other pages in a related group.

Unlike browsing a book, which is linear in design, a Web author can never be sure what other pages the reader has seen before linking to the current page. Graphics placed above the main heading should not be so large that they force the title of the page on a standard monitor (640 × 480 pixels) to go off the screen.

- *Footers*. Ideally, each page should have a footer that contains your name, organization, navigational elements (links or icons), copyright information, and revision/change dates.
- *Contact information*. Like any fine work of art, a good Web page should have a signature or some other form of contact information. You can provide a link to your e-mail that will automatically open the student's e-mail program to send comments and feedback to you.
- *Navigation*. Include a target (a return link) to your top level on each page so readers have a quick way of returning to the beginning. It also helps to include links to an index, a glossary, or table of contents, other sections, and previous and next pages. You might want to add these targets to the bottom of the page, so the learner always knows where to find them. If your links only flow downward from the home page, the pages in your document will become dead ends.
- *Links*. Avoid the "click here" syndrome when defining a link; for example, "Get information about whatever is available by clicking here." Learners then have to remember where they're going once they jump to another page. It's better to link to words or phrases that are a meaningful part of a sentence; for example, "Information about building links." If you use links to items on the same page, remember to use relative links, as absolute links (full URLs) can cause a browser to reload the page each time a link is selected.
- *Time stamps*. Date your revisions and indicate those pages that have been changed or are new additions. This is usually placed in the page footer.

It may seem that there is a lot to remember when designing effective Web pages. The key is to spend time planning and developing your template. That template will then serve as a style sheet for all pages within your course. Even if you use a CMS system (e.g. WebCT) you must still devise a course template for consistency within the management system.

Using interaction to enhance learning

Since leaving a Web page is as easy as clicking the mouse button, too often new designers focus their attention exclusively on what attracts and retains the attention of the casual browser. The use of graphics, color, animation, and sound do provide external stimuli to arouse attention – at least momentarily. However, these ultimately do not provide motivation, nor will they maintain learner attention. Attention, and thereby motivation, are best stimulated through interaction. A page bereft of graphics, sound, and multimedia can still provide excellent teaching and learning benefits because the student is invited to interact.

Interaction requires significantly more than clicking a mouse and following a hyperlink; it requires involvement in higher-order thinking skills such as synthesis, application, and interpretation. This type of interaction can be encouraged through inquiry, in which learners encounter a problem, contradictory information, or a mystery to be resolved. Other methods include establishing the relevance or value of the material for the users (e.g. asking them to reflect and write about its use in their work environment) or by having the students generate links to related information or direct application. The key is designing the course so that the learner must *actively* process and make sense of the information presented. It is only during interaction that learning actually takes place.

Interaction occurs on four levels:

- Interaction with the content.
- Interaction with the instructor.
- Interaction with classmates.
- Interaction with self.

As a course designer, you have a great deal of control over the first two types of interaction, and some control over the third type. However, you have no control over the interaction students experience with themselves – comparing new knowledge with old, generalizing mental models, selecting and disgarding information – the act of cognition. Nevertheless, by designing the first three levels of interaction you can help to ensure that the student's mental processing is more likely to select concepts and methods that you deem important to the learning scenario.

Interaction with content

As stated above, interaction requires more than hyperlinks and clicking from one piece of content to another. For the student to interact with content, you must

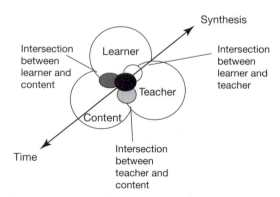

Figure 5.3 Intersection of learning and teacher control over time. Conference presentation, from McVay (1998), reproduced by permission

consider how to design the content so that it can provide guidance and feedback. This feedback can be provided either during the learners' exploration of Web material or afterward, by critiquing the representations of their exploration. For example, during the exploration of course Web pages, many hyperlinks are simply shown by highlighted text in which the text itself serves as a descriptor for the topic. Users will tell you, however, that often these descriptors turn out to be misleading or even irrelevant. This is particularly true when an instructor lists perhaps ten links and asks the student to select three to read, or, worse, the instructor links to a meta-site that provides a plethora of hyperlinks with no helpful annotation or categorization scheme. A more meaningful system would be to present your links in a guided fashion with categorizations such as "definition," "example," or "non-example" when teaching concepts or principles, and "defined path," "shortest path," or "alternative path(s)" when teaching a procedure.

Another method to develop interaction with content is to give several opportunities for learner self-assessment. This can be done through quick questions or mini-tests that provide immediate feedback but are not recorded in grades or limited to the number of attempts. If these types of interactions are used to determine appropriate or inappropriate responses by the learner, pages linked to their answers can be used to either reinforce the correct response or explain the rationale of an incorrect answer and guide the user to a more appropriate answer or other remediation. Increasing the sophistication of this type of content interaction would include CGI or Javascripts (available in most CMS systems) that can analyze responses and give detailed information and alternative choices. Feedback can be as specific as the designer wishes to code and provide individual students with deeper explanations of the consequences of their choices. Simulations and expert systems are the most complex example of this type of content interaction; in these applications the program captures learner variables and "reacts" by presenting additional scenarios based on those variables.

Interaction with the instructor

Less software-dependent but more time-consuming during the delivery of the course is interacting with the instructor. As discussed previously, in the online environment the instructor becomes a mentor to the student. Students need to feel comfortable capitalizing on that mentorship relationship. The instructor can help build a feeling of ease and trust by implementing six design facets in the course and by the manner in which he or she models these facets in response to student queries.

* *Articulate a shared goal.* State the course goal clearly in the syllabus or at the beginning of each unit, then encourage students to mold the goal to their application. Try to find a compromise that will meet both course and students' needs.
* *Set a tone of mutual respect, tolerance, and trust.* The teacher sets this tone, from the initial welcome letter through every communication, be it e-mail, discussion board posting, or student feedback. Furthermore, the manner in

which the instructor deals with (or doesn't deal with) disruptive students will also set the tone.

*   *Provide continual but not continuous communication.* Communication comes in many forms: through Web pages, postings, e-mail, etc. The instructor pre-selects the manner in which he or she will communicate throughout the class. It is impossible and certainly not desirable to be always available to students (though it sometimes seems that is their expectation). It is important that the types and timing of instructor communication are clear to the learner. For example, if you answer e-mail only three times per week, then you need to make a statement to the students like "I will be responding to your e-mails on Tuesday, Thursday, and Saturday." Nothing is more frustrating to a student than expecting an immediate response and not getting one, or, worse, having feedback promised for a particular time and not receiving the feedback or a response identifying a new time frame.
*   *Offer and encourage both formal and informal environments.* The information on Web pages, the essay assignments from students, and perhaps the opening letter are all formal environments. Most students understand this, but it doesn't hurt to reiterate them. Also offer informal environments through discussion board postings, chat rooms, and other contexts. Modeling an informal mode of communication will help the students feel more comfortable doing the same. One way to do this is to engage in some self-disclosure when in an informal environment. For example, when starting your chat office hours you might take time to chat about hobbies, the weather, or an upcoming holiday before getting into the question and answer period.
*   *Do not always expect or desire consensus.* The instructor is the final arbiter in all decisions. Though it is valuable to have students take ownership of certain things – like group work assignments – it is important that students clearly understand how evaluations and assessments will be done. Also, in the case of interpersonal difficulty among students, it will still remain the instructor's responsibility to arbitrate.
*   *Create a sense of "social presence" online.* Physical presence is often men-tioned as a problem with online courses. This does not need to be the case if a sense of "social presence" has been established. This is done by providing opportunities for social knowledge, interaction, and self-disclosure. Techniques such as student biographies, pictures posted to a shared page, shared e-mail addresses, and allowing "small talk" at the beginning of synchronous activities all help to build this social presence. As discussed in a previous chapter on building learning community, it is this social presence that generates comments from online students such as "I felt closer to my classmates online than I ever did in a regular classroom – even though I never physically met them."

Interaction with classmates

Humans are a social species, and particularly in the Web-based environment it is important to provide opportunities for this natural tendency to operate. This is done with small group activities. A small group is defined as learners working together in groups of two to eight to discuss, question, pursue problems cooperatively, and report. Not only do small groups provide an opportunity for socialization and building on the social presence previously described, but they also present an opportunity for students to synthesize the content and improve their communication skills.

Kemp *et al.* (1998) identified several strengths and limitations of small group formats (*Designing Effective Instruction*, second edition, Kemp *et al.* Data reproduced by permission of John Wiley and Sons, Inc.). These would apply equally to both the traditional and online environments.

Strengths

- A small group format can engender synthesis of content by allowing individuals to discuss materials, share ideas, and problem-solve with others.
- Learners acquire experiences in listening and oral expression through reacting to others' ideas and presenting their own.
- By listening to (reading) student discussions in a small group session, an instructor can gain increased awareness of the successes or shortcomings of various phases of an instructional program.
- Small groups promote active learning.
- Learners develop social skills by working with others.

Limitations

- Students need to complete assigned readings before the small group activities so that they will be ready to participate.
- Instructors who are not prepared or who are inexperienced with small group activities may fall back on lecturing for their own security or provide too much input at the expense of the discussion.
- Careful planning of group composition and management are required to create an atmosphere that encourages all group members to participate.
- Individual groups require feedback on their progress and often prompting to help them cover the planned information.
- Students are not trained instructors; thus the group activities should be used to supplement rather than replace other forms of instruction.

A number of different techniques can be used to encourage interaction within small groups:

- *Discussions* can take place either synchronously (chat rooms, telephone or video-conferencing) or asynchronously (discussion board). They are an opportunity for facts, ideas, and opinions to be exchanged. The discussions can be moderated by the instructor or centered in the group itself. They can be formal and graded or informal and only participation is counted. The instructor sets the tone and must articulate the format.
- *Case studies* provide learners with detailed information about a real-life situation. All related circumstances, issues, and actions of persons involved are

carefully described. Students then study and analyze the situation as presented. They decide what was done correctly and what mistakes might have been avoided. In some case studies the students may be asked to solve the problem presented. Case studies, like discussions, may be done synchronously or asynchronously.

- *Role-playing and simulation* allow spontaneous reactions and problem-solving by two or more learners. Each person takes on and acts out a role as he or she feels it would be played in real life. Depending on the scenario, other learners may observe and report or the entire small group may be enmeshed in the dramatization, undergoing the same stress and pressures they would experience in reality. If all group members are role-playing, then the instructor discusses and evaluates the results. These are most often done synchronously (chat or MOO/MUD or virtual world). However, it is also possible to do this asynchronously through a time-limited discussion board activity (e.g. everyone must post responses and play out role and problem-solving within forty-eight hours from the commencement of the simulation).
- *Games* are formalized simulation activities where two or more participants or teams compete in attempting to meet a set of objectives relating to the topic. Depending on the goal, games may be synchronous or asynchronous. They may be as simple as looking at a picture and "guessing" the number of objects (to later demonstrate conformity or authority) to as complex as the type of games sold for entertainment with points and defined winners and losers.

Whatever cooperative learning format is selected, it is important to plan well in advance what concepts will be reinforced, what group and individual rewards will be granted, what type of accountability you will expect, and how you will ensure equal opportunity for success. The primary student complaint about any type of group activity is accountability of individuals versus that of the group. Therefore it is very important to have a clear and well articulated plan regarding assessment of any group activities.

Interaction with self

The one part of interaction that teachers have no control over is the act of cognition – interaction with self through reflection, comparison, and generalization or special-ization of knowledge. However, you can encourage this type of interaction in your course design by specifying time for self-interaction and asking students to share that process as much as possible; the primary tool is reflection. Reflection can be encouraged on a continual basis throughout a project, such as asking students to post quick thoughts or reactions regarding statements; or can be encouraged after certain concepts or after the completion of a course. These latter reflections are often used to help the students summarize and apply their learning or realize how far they have come in their knowledge.

Three formats are most common to use for reflection:

- *Personal journals* usually kept throughout a course and used to reflect on knowledge, problems, or applications. The journals may be submitted at the end of learning units or concept modules, or at the end of the course to show the continuous process of reflection and learning.

- *Reflection essays* assigned to focus on a particular process or concept, or to reflect on the course at completion. Sometimes these essays may also provide information to the instructor about what went well and what needs to be improved, as well as what the students found most interesting or motivational.

- *Reflection postings* used particularly in courses where correct and incorrect responses may not be well defined (e.g. ethics, religious studies, political analysis, etc.). These are usually generated by the instructor posting a dilemma or statement to the discussion board and asking students to reflect on the item and post feelings, experiences, or applications.

Whatever type of reflection interaction you build into your course, it can truly bring the "big picture" together for students as they learn new concepts. Reflection gives learners an opportunity to articulate to themselves and/or to you how they are generalizing their mental models to incorporate the new knowledge. It is a great way for instructors to get a snapshot of the applicability of the knowledge at that moment and to adapt course material and activities for the future. As the course is not face-to-face, and often students involved in Web-based courses are very busy people, taking time for reflection is not usually high on learners' priority lists. Thus it is up to the instructor to ensure this important self-interaction takes place.

Materials that support Web-based courses

New online designers sometimes make the mistake of attempting to develop a course that uses only materials available on the Web. The belief of these new designers seems to be that it will be easier for the students to access materials, and it will allow them a wide range of search functions. Both of these assumptions are true. However, limiting the entire instruction to the Web also limits the effectiveness of the learning experience to a small number of activities and students. Just as you use a variety of media in a classroom, so also should you expect to use a variety of media in your Web-based courses.

Contrary to popular belief, textbooks are not going to disappear in the Web-based classroom environment. In fact, many students truly appreciate having a textbook to supplement their learning. The textbook provides a different way of organizing information, as well as a kinesthetic tool for many learners. One complaint about materials available only on the Web is that students cannot read or learn when away from the computer. Many institutions have reported that students print 95 percent of the material they find on the Web so they can have the pages with them as they travel to work, on trips, or wait for services. This is where the textbook becomes an important partner to your course design.

Other text-based supplements to your online course include articles, instructor notes, and assignments. In fact, there is an ongoing controversy among educators as to whether it is better to place all text materials online or to distribute them as a course packet along with the textbook. If students are going to print all of the online material anyway, there is good reason to avoid putting so much text online and simply supplying it to your learners in the format they prefer. On the other hand, some designers would argue that having all the text online allows better search, hyperlinking, and tracking of student use. The point is not to dismiss the possibility of having additional text-based paper elements that the student purchases or receives that are referred to online but not duplicated.

Though technology now allows us to develop streaming video, quick time movies, and large audio files to be delivered over the Web, it doesn't mean that this is the best way to deliver the material. Bandwidth is still a huge issue for most students accessing their courses from a home or business computer. This is particularly true in rural areas and in countries where the infrastructure is not fully developed. Someone accessing the Web with a 56k modem (the typical speed at this writing) will have many problems downloading audio, video and quick time movies. In some cases, the video will not play at all. In others, the video plays but the audio is not synchronized because of latency. Also, if the video signal is received the latency makes it difficult to view or to evaluate. If presenting video or audio is an important element in your course, you are better advised to use a CD.

Like textbooks, CDs are an important media partner to course design. A CD can hold a great deal of material. You can stream audio, video, tutorials, and a variety of other material to a CD and the student will see it exactly as you prepared it without all the problems of dialing in with their modem. Within your Web-based course you can instruct your students to put in their CD, watch a movie clip, and then respond on the discussion board as you deem appropriate. In this way, you have provided good instruction and can still guide the students' experience and understanding of the content, even though it is not delivered directly from your Web site. Audio and video tapes are still viable media partners, as are several other presentational tools.

The key to selecting media is to follow the same rules that guide all course design: first define the goals and objectives, then determine the best means by which to teach the material and assess mastery. Selecting media based on this rule will always assure the best course development possible.

Instructional strategies

The status of the Web as an alternative instruction delivery mechanism is already focusing educators on how to foster creative, critical, and cooperative student processes. According to Torrance (1972), creativity requires students to sense gaps in information, make guesses and hypotheses, test and revise ideas, and communicate results. All of these are part of, or lead to, higher-order thinking skills. In an extensive review of creativity in research, Bonk and Reynolds (1996) also found that the Web supported students in breaking away from the norms of the learning process. They found that using the Web nurtured the following key attributes found in most creative people.

- Willingness to take risks
- Commitment to task
- Curiosity
- Openness to experience
- Broad interests
- Originality
- Imaginative play
- Intuition
- Attraction to novelty and complexity
- Artistic ability
- Metaphorical thinking
- Problem-finding
- Elaboration of ideas

The key to capturing this creative knowledge-building is the role the teacher takes in managing this sharing, as well as scaffolding these efforts with comments and suggestions that guide and intellectually support the learner during his or her quest for knowledge mastery. Many of the approaches that work in the classroom for generating creativity and managing scaffolding also work on the Web.

Similar cognitive activities are presented in Table 5.1, but the emphasis is changed according to the type of thinking and learning that is desired. It is also possible to combine emphases in a single exercise. For example, in row 1 you might have students brainstorm in small groups, then categorize their ideas, and finally have the entire class use a nominal process to vote or rank the items as to applicability or importance. In other instances, you may elect to use only one category of activity.

In the next chapter, a more detailed explanation of specific Web-based tools will be covered (i.e. e-mail, chat rooms, discussion boards, audio/video streaming, etc.). However, before selecting these tools, it is wise to understand how they are used and to determine which tools you may want to use in your classes. One way to begin this process is take a moment to list all the things that take place in the classroom environment (e.g. discussions, role-playing, case studies, question-and-answer sessions, and assignments). Then formulate a plan for incorporating all those same interactions into the Web-based environment. Table 5.2 depicts how you can translate those classroom-based types of interactions to your Web-based distance education environment.

Feedback mechanisms

The crux of most assessment comes from homework assignments. In the online environment, assignments are usually sent as an e-mail attachment in whatever format is required – wordprocessed documents, spreadsheets, picture files for scanned documents. When faced with all these attachments, some teachers immediately begin to question how they will give appropriate feedback in this new environment. The days of collecting papers in class, manually marking them and

Table 5.1 Thinking and learning

Creative thinking	Critical thinking	Cooperative learning
Brainstorming – the wilder the better and no evaluation	Categorization schemes – create taxonomies or contrast matrices	Value lines or voting/ranking of concepts
What if or just suppose – science fiction or fairy-tale thinking	Case-based reasoning	Partner activities – share, check, review, tell and retell ideas
Creative writing: telling tall tales – begin a story on the topic and ask students to complete it	Problem vignettes	Asynchronous conferencing, message posting to share ideas, tales, vignette applications
Role-play thinking – assign roles to a case study (e.g. judge, inventor, idea squelcher, idea generator, devil's advocate, optimist, etc.)	Critiques, rebuttals around posted topics or role-play situations	Structured controversy – pairs of students assigned pro and con sides
Simulations – assign specific character roles for application of knowledge (e.g. teacher, parent, administrator, politician, etc.)	Mock trials, debates, posted arguments with logic delineated	Problem-based group learning – students work together to create a product or solve a problem
Analogy builder – students complete analogies. A good online teacher is like a . . . (e.g. director, artist, preacher, etc.)	Summaries, reviews, abstracts	Gallery tours – each small group of students create a summary or shared page of work around a theme
Personal journals/ reflective papers – write notes after class, reflect on entire course, time-limited writing	Minute papers and reflection logs – use guided questions to stimulate thinking	Individual posted journal with encouraged comments by other students who had same experience
Mind mapping – free association map with a concept's attributes and characteristics	Build graphic organizers – flow charts, decision-making trees, concept maps	Synchronous conferencing with a whiteboard – all students add to ideas to graphic
Question lists – for spurring ideas around the topic (e.g. What can you add? Delete? How would the President have handled that? etc.)	Students devise questions for self-test or mid-term and final exams. Learners lead Q&A session on specified topics	Group investigation – divide topics among groups and have each investigate then present to entire class

returning them the next week seem far away. Certainly, you would still have the option of marking papers and returning them to students via the postal service. However, this is neither efficient nor what students expect. The expectation is for you to provide feedback electronically – to send them a marked copy as an e-mail

Table 5.2 Translation of classroom-based interactions to the Web

Classroom interaction	Form of Web interaction	Description of potential use
Class discussions	Chat – synchronous, immediate interactivity	Schedule specific chat times when students may gather to discuss a topic. It is useful to structure the chat by providing questions or topics in advance.
	Bulletin board – asynchronous, gives time for considered responses	Post questions on the bulletin board and ask for student responses.
Role-playing	MOOs/MUDs (multi-user dimensions)	Students come to chat in assigned roles; a scenario can be previously posted on a Web page.
Case studies	Chat	Provide case study in advance (via textbook or Web pages) and ask students to come prepared to chat.
	Bulletin board	Post specific case-related questions to bulletin board.
	E-mail	Ask for a written, analytical assignment to be attached to e-mail.
Question-and-answer sessions	Bulletin board	Designate a topic on the bulletin board for questions and answers.
	Chat	Have chat office hours posted in advance. It is advisable to pick at least two differing times (e.g. Saturday 8.00 a.m. and Wednesday 9.00 p.m.); remember geographical time differences within your student population.
Assignments and peer critiques	E-mail attachment	Send attachments to the instructor via e-mail for grading and feedback.
	Web page	Post to Web and send URL to instructor.
	Bulletin board posting	Cut and paste to bulletin board for sharing with entire class; you may also use peer critique with this method.

attachment. Fortunately, there are now a number of tools you can use to provide feedback in just this manner.

A wonderful device is the electronic editing tool provided by some word-processing programs. For example, Microsoft Word has a special toolbar for editing called the Reviewing toolbar. This toolbar offers two ways to edit a wordprocessed document – tracking changes or writing notes. See Figures 5.4–5.

Using the Track Changes function in Microsoft Word. Whenever you make a change it crosses out the previous entry and adds your change (Figure 5.4). In this

This is an example of a ~~correctable thing~~correction using the track changes function in Microsoft Word

Figure 5.4 The Track Changes function in Microsoft Word

way students can see both what they wrote and your suggested changes, which appear in a different color. Even without the use of a package like Microsoft Word, you could accomplish some of this same functionality by simply typing in your comments in a different font color using any common wordprocessing package.

Using the Comments function in Microsoft Word. You highlight the item on which you wish to comment and select the "sticky note" icon. A dialogue box appears where you type in your comments. When the user receives the document with your feedback, simply placing the mouse cursor on the highlighted area will pop-up your comments in a box as depicted in Figure 5.5. Again, without the use of a tool like this you could still provide your comments electronically by typing them in a different color and selecting a protocol you will consistently use and articulate to your students. For example, you might say, "All my comments will be typed in red letters and enclosed in parentheses."

example pictures below

Newuser:
Nice phrasing for this example. You should do this more often.

This is an example of a highlighted item with comments using Microsoft Word.

Figure 5.5 The Comments function in Microsoft Word

Some CMS systems provide a shared environment where students may place all of their homework assignments. These are then translated as Web pages and you use the fonts and colors available to that environment to do your editing. Then the students retrieve them from that shared space for their review. There are numerous variations on this same theme of electronically editing. The point is to find an effective way to provide feedback to your students. This same type of mechanism may also be used by your students to do peer critiques of papers.

In addition to papers, always remember to provide feedback on other interactive items where the student is being assessed. If you are moderating a discussion in chat, be sure to provide some comments at the end of the chat (or as the discussion is in progress). Minimally, summarize the points and reinforce the participation time the students put in. If you are reviewing postings on a discussion board, be sure to post your pointers there as well. Students appreciate knowing that you are, in fact, reading their work. They want to know if they are progressing satisfactorily and what you are looking for in their responses. No one wants to be surprised by his or her grade.

Finally, grades are important to students. If you are using a CMS system that provides an accessible grade book, be sure your students understand how to access their records and keep the assignment grades up to date. If your system does not provide that functionality, then be sure to take the time to at least e-mail grade progress at selected times during the term. For example, in a ten-week term you might e-mail progress grades at the fifth week and again at the eighth week. In a longer term, you might elect to mail them three or four times. As with all assignments and feedback in the Web-based environment the key is to accurately set the students' expectations by articulating what you want and how you will provide comments.

Maintaining quality

Designing, developing, maintaining, and delivering a quality course is certainly time-consuming. However, it is also rewarding on both personal and institutional levels. Once the initial investment in course development is made, the course can be used again and again with changes incorporated when needed. Developing your course using discrete elements (objects) that can be removed or shared will enhance the ease of maintenance. The key is to keep quality issues at the top of your list during the entire development and maintenance process.

The National Education Association (NEA) in the United States partnered with Blackboard Inc. to commission a policy study on quality benchmarks for distance learning in higher education. To formulate these benchmarks, the study contacted leaders in online distance education and asked for examples of practical strategies they used or found effective. The benchmarks relating to course development and teaching/learning are reproduced below.

- Guidelines regarding minimum standards are used for course development, design, and delivery, while learning outcomes – not the availability of existing technology – determine the technology being used to deliver course content.
- Instructional materials are reviewed periodically to ensure they meet program standards.
- Intended learning outcomes are reviewed regularly to ensure clarity, utility, and appropriateness.
- Courses are designed to require students to engage in analysis, synthesis, and evaluation as part of their course and program requirements.
- Students are provided with supplemental course information that outlines course objectives, concepts, and ideas; learning outcomes for each course are summarized in a clearly written, straightforward statement.
- Faculty and students agree upon expectations regarding times for student assignment completion and faculty response.
- Student interaction with faculty and other students is an essential characteristic and is facilitated through a variety of ways, including voice mail and/or e-mail.
- Feedback to student assignments and questions is constructive and provided in a timely manner.
- Students are instructed in the proper methods of effective research, including assessment of the validity of resources.

- The program's educational effectiveness and teaching/learning process are assessed through an evaluation process that uses several methods and applies specific standards.

Benchmarks provide a vehicle for measuring and guiding your progress in designing, developing, delivering, and maintaining quality online courses. As your program emerges, you may wish to add additional points of reference that specifically reflect your student population or the curriculum you are offering online. Finally, you will have a clear path established to evaluate your course, student learning, and needed changes throughout the life cycle of your development.

6 Selecting Web-based tools

Too often, institutions begin their Web-based development process by selecting the tools first, then allowing the tools to determine the pedagogy. This method leads to courses and processes that are dictated by technology instead of using technology to enhance the learning process. The selection of tools should come well after determining your need, your understanding of how you want to develop courses, and your practice with online teaching. The tools you select should reflect your specific environment, technical capabilities, and strategic plans for your information systems future. Also, the tools you select need to provide some room for growth and change (scalability).

Web-based system tools should be selected in much the same way you would choose any new software system. First, make a list of pertinent questions and answer them before asking for competitive bids or prior to beginning your shopping. Of course, the big question to answer first is "What do I plan to do with this system?" Is it to offer courses at a distance with no face-to-face time? Is it to enhance classroom-based courses? Is it to simply provide a Web presence for your school? Is it a combination of uses? Once the big question is answered, break it down into the subsystems you may need to address:

- *Information distribution.* Will information be distributed only via the Web? If so, what browser support are you willing to offer? Will information be also distributed via e-mail? Who (students, faculty, staff) will be allowed to distribute information?
- *Communication.* What types of communication do you want to encourage in your Web-based courses (e-mail, discussion boards, chats, whiteboards, audio/video)? Who will have access to, or control over, the communications? Will the communications require special software for users to obtain or download? Who will support the software?
- *Student assessment.* What different types of assessment do you want available to the Web-based environment (multiple choice, true/false, fill-in-the blank, essay, reflection)? Do you want the grading of assessments to be manual, automatic, overridable, available for viewing?
- *Course, teacher, and program assessment.* Do you want your Web-based system to perform any analysis of evaluation forms, system use, individual

logins? Where or to whom will such information be sent? Who will be allowed to view it?

• *Class management*. How do you want to handle student additions, drops, section changes? Do you want the capability to simultaneously update multiple classes at once? How do you want to manage student information such as grades, participation, logins, biographies, promotion? What type of student tracking would you like?

• *Integration with other student/faculty support systems*. Do you want the students to be automatically enrolled in the appropriate online classes when they register? How do you want to create your student management database? Do you plan to offer online counseling, advising, tutoring? Will students be able to register, get financial aid, view transcripts online? Will course information be linked with faculty information such as biographies, office hours, contact information?

Determining the answers to the subsystem questions will help you resolve whether you should purchase an integrated system or provide a common interface for several individual systems that meet your specific needs.

Comparing tools

Most communication tools require the installation and maintenance of a server program that manages and distributes the communication. The traditional approach is to obtain and install the necessary server programs on your institution's computer(s). Both the installation and the maintenance of the server-side tools usually require knowledgeable technical personnel and can become a time-demanding responsibility, particularly for smaller institutions, or those who have not developed a large technical infrastructure. The cost of installation and maintenance can outweigh the benefit gained from using it.

An alternative that has become quite popular is to use someone else's server and technical personnel. There are a number of commercial sites that offer such a service, and some larger universities (for a fee) will host smaller colleges on their server. Your decision to buy and maintain the server communication software yourself, or to rent it and use someone else's hosting services, should be based on the relative costs and benefits associated with each choice. When making that determination, keep capabilities and cost in mind.

• *Capabilities*. Your chosen tool and hosting mechanisms should provide all the capabilities you require now and for future versions of your Web-based environment. Aim for balance between what you need now and the widest range of possibilities in the future. Scalability is very important. Once you have adopted a tool and have it in widespread use, moving to another tool can be both time-consuming and costly. It is important to choose carefully.

• *Cost*. Internet communication software is available in four price ranges: free, shareware, educational discount, and commercial. There is usually no correlation between the price charged for a tool and its quality. In fact, many of the free communication tools have great advantages over their commercial competitors. The primary differences between many free or shareware and commercial packages are the user interface, the modification capabilities, and the ease of use in terms of installation and maintenance. Sometimes the free packages require more technical capability on the server side to install and modify. Usually the client software interface is as easy to use in free packages as in commercial packages.

If you decide to pay for a tool, price should not be the only consideration. Training in the use and management of a tool, combined with the cost of modifying or maintaining it, contributes a far greater proportion of the software's cost. Keeping this in mind, you should evaluate the following issues when looking at a vendor:

Support

- Is it provided by the software manufacturer?
- If support is local, is it provided by telephone?
- Is it free or does it have added costs?

Upgrades

- How often are upgrades made?
- Are they compatible upward and downward with existing versions?
- What are the likely costs?

Technical skill level

- What is required to install and maintain the software?
- Do you have personnel with those skills already or will you have to hire additional staff?
- If you have to hire additional staff, how does that cost factor into the decision to purchasing the tool?

Server, client, and network requirements

- What is needed for running the tool effectively?
- Is the tool platform-dependent (e.g. UNIX, Mac, PC)?
- Do you get the source code to modify or are you stuck with whatever interface and links they provide?

Information distribution

The Web has become the largest shared repository of information in the world. Though it began as a storehouse of text-based resources, it has now also become a repository for discussions, graphics, video, music, and a variety of other media.

Using this storage capability, you can make available for your students or your peers any type of media: sound files containing speeches, video clips showing real demonstrations, animations of processes, and various types of pictures. You can combine these media to provide specific learning opportunities, or you can make them available as individual objects for sharing and manipulating in other courses.

In selecting appropriate information distribution tools, you need to ask what distribution options you wish to have available to your Web-based environment.

- Distribution of text and media
- Using the Web-based system for presentations independent of computer platform
- Dynamic publishing – the ability to add to a course or make changes on the fly
- Administrative information
- Resource and reference material
- Searchable information
- Personal/shared space

Depending on what you select, a variety of assets will be needed.

Viewing tools

The browser is the primary viewing tool for the Web. Unfortunately, it is not feasible to discuss every type of browser. With the possible complexities of code these days, you can no longer simply put up an HTML page and trust it will be accessible to everyone. It is best to select one or two browsers that you are willing to support and make that information readily available to all potential users. For example, if you decide to support Netscape and Internet Explorer, then you must test your course pages on each browser to make sure they view the same. However, don't assume that these same pages are equally viewable on AOL's browser or other proprietary systems.

Beyond the browser, you may have a number of other required viewers depending on your content, links to outside sites, and what types of information students may need to distribute. Many people choose to make research papers or instructor notes available in Postscript (PS) or Portable Document Format (PDF). These formats do not automatically display in a Web browser; they require a special viewer, such as Adobe Acrobat for PDF files or GhostScript for PS files. Like browsers, both these file types can be read (using the right viewer) on both PC and Mac platforms.

If you plan to use other media, for instance video clips, another viewer is required. You must determine what format to use for these clips – quick time or real video. Much information is distributed over the Web directly from other applications, for example Microsoft PowerPoint or Word. Each of these requires yet another viewer. Viewers are handy in that they allow others to look at your documents without having to actually own the software. In this way, you can share your PowerPoint presentation even with those who don't have PowerPoint software, because the viewer allows others to see it, but not change it.

Browser and viewer resources

- Netscape: http://www.netscape.com/
- Internet Explorer: http://www.microsoft.com/windows/ie/default.htm
- Adobe Acrobat: http://www.adobe.com/prodindex/acrobat/readstep.html
- GhostScript: http://www.cs.wisc.edu/~ghost/
- Quick Time: http://www.apple.com/quicktime/download/
- Real Player: http://scopes.real.com/real/player/
- Microsoft Office viewers: http://www.microsoft.com/office/000/viewers.htm
- Shockwave: http://www.macromedia.com/shockwave/download/

Reference materials

Reference materials distribution is available via electronic library access. Librarians have been at the forefront of electronic distribution for some time now. In fact, in many colleges and universities it is the librarians who have provided the impetus for moving to a Web-based learning environment. Many libraries now provide a collection of electronic resources to students, faculty, staff, and sometimes alumni. These electronic collections include databases, library catalogs, online journals and newspapers, and Internet resources. These come in three primary formats:

- *Access to the library catalog* of books, journals, and other references. The user selects the item he or she requires, then requests it be sent via mail, fax, or as an e-mail attachment. Many libraries will scan and fax or e-mail short articles in the collection. Books and longer articles are generally sent via regular mail.
- *Access to abstracts* that describe the reference and provide locator numbers to assist the librarian in getting the information. ERIC is a typical example of this type of reference material. Also, several electronic databases have a combination of full-text articles and abstracted articles. The abstracts need to be part of the library's collection or obtained through interlibrary loan when possible.
- *Student electronic access to full-text databases*. These databases provide the actual reference item in full text online or deliver them via an e-mail attachment. Many popular academic journals, magazines, and some monographs or dissertations are available via this full-text format. This type of access is timely, easily searchable, and saves on book storage costs.

Among some of the most popular larger electronic databases are:

- ProQuest.
- Wilson Select.
- ABI Inform.
- First Search.
- InfoTrak.
- ERIC.

There are literally hundreds of database types and research capabilities. If you are just getting started, it may be helpful to select a couple of the large databases mentioned above that provide both abstracts and full text. Determine which journals and types of materials you need to have available online and build your collection from there.

Searchable materials

Determine what method you would like to use to find materials on your site. You can draw on a variety of indexing programs and utilities to make it easy for users to search all the information you distribute on the Web. This saves time and prevents frustration in navigating the complexities of multiple pages and directory structures. A number of free indexers or search engines exist in addition to commercial products. Several organizations provide good information about indexing and searching via the Web.

- UKOLN: http://www.ukoln.ac.uk/Web-focus/activities/searching/
- TERENA Task Force: http://www.terena.nl/task-forces/tf-chic/library.html
- American Society of Indexers: http://www.asindexing.org/software.shtml

Communication tools

Most educators recognize the importance of human interaction to the learning process. The use of Web-based communication tools addresses this need in the online environment. As with the information distribution tools, prior to selecting communication tools you need to determine how you plan to use them and to what extent. There are three types of Web-based communications to consider: asynchronous text/graphic communication, synchronous text/graphic communication, and simulated face-to-face communication. The question is: which tools will let you achieve the desired outcome? The question for the Web systems designer is whether to select a variety of individual tools or to purchase an integrated system.

This section will cover individual tools you might select to combine and integrate as a hybrid course management system. The advantage to these individual tools is twofold: (1) each tool was designed to do only one or two things and therefore does it very well; (2) many of these individual tools are free to educational institutions, making start-up costs much more affordable. With a good interface design, these free tools could be incorporated into an overall Web-based system for little cost and a great deal of reward.

A plethora of tools are currently available to incorporate communication into a Web-based course environment. Rather than attempt to list and discuss each one, this chapter will briefly describe how each works, and then provide a tools table with a brief description of the tool, what features to evaluate, and a listing of a few of the most popular free tools used by educational institutions.

Asynchronous text/graphic communication

E-mail and threaded discussion boards are the tools most used to facilitate user communication without the need to be online at the same time. Students and teachers participate as their schedules allow or within specified time frames.

E-mail

E-mail is a major form of personal communication on the Internet. An individual reads, composes, and sends e-mail using a program called a mail user agent. E-mail programs are available in two types: server and client. E-mail servers fulfill the role of message delivery, routing, and storage. Usually, an educational institution provides the server hardware and software. Users then employ a program that matches their installation. Free Web-based e-mail clients have now emerged (e.g. hotmail). These services provide users with free e-mail addresses and a Web-based server. However, be aware that these accounts generate their income by advertising to the people who use them.

Mailing lists

Mailing lists are used to specifically support the creation and delivery of e-mail between individuals in a predetermined group. Though these lists make it easy to distribute common messages, they also come with additional tasks that must be assigned to someone: membership management, archive maintenance, and message delivery (automatic or moderated). Lists have traditionally required users to issue specific commands to interact with the list (e.g. subscribe, unsubscribe). Though not difficult, for many members it is annoying. To combat this problem, some lists have created a Web-based interface for mailing list management. These interfaces usually provide a form page that can be filled out by the user and, through a Web/e-mail gateway, it will automatically issue the appropriate commands and deliver the e-mail.

News readers

News readers, including Usenet, provide a collection of asynchronous, text-based discussion forums. These operate very much like threaded discussion boards. These newsgroups have now archived thousands of topics ranging from computer science to religion and are widely used in education. Users access these collections with readers to peruse and post news articles on the Web. News servers are programs that store and forward news articles. Each news server accepts a subset of newsgroups and deletes articles after a specified period of time. It is common for a news server to contain a number of local newsgroups that no other server stores.

Threaded discussions

Threaded discussions have long been used as an effective text-based communication tool for conferencing. The use of these tools in education began on mainframes in

Table 6.1 Asynchronous text/graphic communication

Tool	Features to evaluate	Free software
E-mail	Message threading Filtering Address books Attachments Enhanced text	*Client/server* Netscape Communicator Pegasus Eudora Light *Web-based* Yahoo Mail Hotmail Rocket Mail
Mailing lists	Membership management Archive maintenance Message delivery options Web/e-mail gateway options	Majordomo ListProc LWGate Mailserv Pandora Hypermail MHonArc
News readers	Newsgroup creation Newsgroup access Article expiration	Netscape Collabra InterNews Agent INN *Free Web-based services* FeedMe BillyBoard
Threaded discussion boards	Message tracking Shared documents Hyperlink capabilities Graphic incorporation Voting system	CoW WWWBoard Hypernews

the mid-1970s and continues today on the Internet. The years of educational institution experience using these tools led to systems that provide a number of useful facilities such as shared documents, tracking read messages, and voting systems.

Synchronous text/graphic communication

Chats, MUDs/MOOs, and electronic whiteboards are the tools used in synchronous communications. Unlike the asynchronous tools, these require participants to communicate at the same time. These tools are often used for bonding a class, asking for spontaneity in discussion, simulation of complex tasks, or for office hours and tutoring access.

Chat

Chat systems allow two or more people to participate in synchronous, usually text-based, communication, though many of the new tools use multimedia. Most chat tools support multiple discussion areas, often called channels or rooms, and the use of an anonymous nickname. More complex chat tools offer other features, including logging of conversations, support for multimedia, shared whiteboards, and group Web browsing. Chat systems are client/server based. The client presents a friendly interface by which the user communicates. The server is responsible for distributing the contents of the chat to all the participants in the room. Four primary types of chats exist today:

- *Web forms* that provide a graphical forms interface for user inputs. Upon completion, the user presses ENTER or submit, then the page is reloaded for all users.
- *Internet relays*, where participants' typing is directly relayed to all users.
- *Proprietary systems* available only within the confines of one company or organization. These types of systems usually don't interact with other systems, thus providing a closed environment.
- *Avatar systems* where each person is represented by a graphical virtual character instead of just his or her name. Users can move their character around a virtual room and can sometimes portray emotion by changing the graphical representation (see The Palace, http://www.thepalace.com).

MOO/MUD/MUSH

MOO/MUD/MUSH are acronyms for multi-user discussion or simulation programs. A MUD (multiple user discussion) is a computer program that allows Internet users from around the world to connect to it, create fictional characters for themselves, and then interact with other real users as well as computer-generated entities in a virtual environment. Users can explore their virtual world, talk to or perform actions with other human players, roam through virtual areas, solve puzzles, and seek treasures. Because these virtual environments simulate a full world, learning to use them can have a significantly greater learning curve than the other tools previously discussed. This complexity, however, can be transferred to problems requiring simulation of multifaceted situations such as performing surgery, operating a multinational business, flying an airplane, or studying ecology. The best examples of these multi-user objects are commercial games on the market today (e.g. SimCity, Doom, and a variety of history-related games). Participation in a MUD occurs via a MUD client. The simplest client is the standard Telnet text-based application. More complex clients provide full-blown graphical user interfaces that provide advanced features.

Whiteboards

Whiteboards are usually used in conjunction with a chat room. Whiteboards can be used as a freeform drawing tool for making notes, sharing in brainstorming or mind

Table 6.2 Synchronous graphic/text communication

Tool	Features to evaluate	Free software
Chat	Ease of use Loading or reloading time User interface Ease/difficulty of server install and maintenance Availability of transcripts (conversation logs) Anonymity vs. user authentication	Chat mIRC Ewgie
MOO MUD MUSH	Ease of use Required programming Maintenance of worlds and objects Text or graphical interface	CircleMud
Whiteboard	Ease of use Drawing functions Chat integrated with board Transcript log of chat Ability to save and reload whiteboard graphics	GroupBoard NetMeeting

mapping, or for formal real-time presentations of prepared graphical material. Most often the instructor or a student presents the graphic and then discusses it or asks for comments using the attached chat client. The biggest complaint about most whiteboard programs on the market is the difficulty in using the drawing functions with a mouse-based system. Most people find them impractical to use in a real-time environment unless they have attached a pen tablet or some other type of drawing tool to make it feel more natural.

Simulated face-to-face communication

Internet phone and desktop video conferencing, like the text and graphic-based systems mentioned above, also require participants to communicate at the same time. Until recently these systems were rarely used, owing to bandwidth difficulties. But, with many institutions and ancillary sites now having wideband access, they have become more popular. However, be aware that anyone accessing via a dial-up connection may not be able to participate in this type of communication.

In order to work effectively, audio or video communication requires further infrastructure. Students' computers must have sound cards, microphones, appropriate software, and reasonably fast connections to the Internet. For video conferencing both students and the institution will need client software (e.g. CU-SeeMe), a video camera, a high-speed Internet connection, and some type of distribution mechanisms

Table 6.3 Simulated face-to-face communication

Tool	Features to evaluate	Free software
Audio-conferencing	Bandwidth needed Compression issues Latency issues Server and client software use	BSCW TeamWave Workplace
Desktop video conferencing	Server and client software needs Cost and configuration of video cameras Distribution mechanisms	NetMeeting RealAudio CU-SeeMe

– either a video server (reflector) or a multicast protocol that allows the host to send information to a group of machines.

You might ask, "With all these infrastructure needs why would anyone want to use audio or video conferencing online?" The reason is personal touch and familiarity. Seeing and/or hearing each other is important to many students and teachers alike. A solely text-based medium can seem to be impersonal without a lot of work on bonding and community-building. Audio and video conferencing are not tools you want to use every week in an online course, but when used appropriately they do add an important experience that is unlike the text-based tools. Students often report that once they had heard the professor's voice or seen a classmate, they felt they knew the person better. In subsequent text-based sessions (i.e. e-mail, discussion boards or chats) students then participated more fully and stated that the asynchronous communications took on more meaning and personality after they had heard or seen the other participants. For this reason, providing even one audio or video conference early in the course may make a difference to the students' experience and perceptions of the presence of a "personal touch" throughout the remainder of the text-based activities.

In the absence of these tools, you might consider the use of simple phone conferencing for audio contact. Certainly, talking directly to the teacher can make a difference in the student's perception of attention and involvement. When bandwidth or computer speed issues are a problem, judicious use of the phone can make a difference. If possible, schedule one audio conference within the first few weeks of the term. Include several students at the same time (five to eight is a good number) to enhance that "personal touch." Provide an opportunity to hear tone and inflection, and make a personal connection with each student.

Student assessment tools

Assessment is an important aspect of every course. An ideal assessment provides a means to ensure that students meet the outcomes designed for the course. This chapter will not discuss the pros and cons of various assessments, as that is covered in detail in a later chapter. However, we will look at the types of assessments that can be executed online and automatically graded, as well as those that may require manual input. It is also important that these tools allow instructors to give a grade that can be easily viewed by the student.

Assessments serve two purposes: to evaluate students' progress and to help students learn. Assessments may also be used for course and instructor evaluations. Observing and reviewing teaching strategies and Web-based material may lead to improvements and provide alternative means for effectiveness.

Quiz or test

For student evaluation, there are a number of tools that provide objective assessment through the use of online quizzes or tests. This is done through the use of a form, displayed in the students' browser, with questions and spaces where students place their answers. Usually, at the end of the quiz, learners click on a button that submits the results to the computer. In a few moments, the quiz is graded and the results are displayed. The advantage of using a computer-marked quiz is that the learner receives instant feedback. That feedback can be as simple as right or wrong marks, or as complex as advice for remediation, explanations of what they did wrong, and reinforcement for what was correct. Several disadvantages are also associated with using online tests:

- Some faculty rely solely on these tools to measure outcomes, which is not usually an accurate reflection of the learners' capabilities.
- Students may perceive the tools as impersonal.
- The tests may foster a false sense of confidence or failure, depending on their construction and purpose.
- Depending on the software, the nature of the questions and answers may be very restricted.

Quizzes or tests may be presented in a number of ways: multiple choice, true/false, fill-in-the-blank, matching, ranking, and even ones that allow students to draw a picture or a graph. Your feedback may be simple or complex, depending on the amount of time you can spend developing it. Quizzes can be constructed fairly easily using Javascripts with basic form-handling techniques and then string searches for correct answers, followed by if/then/else statements for inserting feedback. This, of course, would require a programmer who is comfortable with Java.

Quiz tools

Another alternative is to use a quiz tool. There are several available, and many are free and can be integrated into your course through the use of simple hyperlinks. Most of these free tools also offer some type of feedback generation, as well as grade book capabilities. Most of them require you to use their server to host the quizzes, and several have advertising associated with them. A few offer a small fee purchase price (usually $200–$500) if you wish to place the tool on your own server. Some of the free quiz tool offerings are listed below.

- *Authoring Tool for Web-based Tests*, Merex Corporation (http://www. merexcorp.com/testauthor/). Allows users to create self-scoring multiple choice tests without knowing any HTML or Javascript.
- *Hot Potatoes*, University of Victoria, British Columbia (http://web.uvic.ca/ hrd/hotpot/). Create interactive multiple choice, short answer, jumbled sentence, crossword, matching or ordering, and gap-fill exercises for the Web.
- *Interactive Test*, University of Copenhagan (http://12teach.com/). Create online multiple choice tests and fill-in-the-blank for free up to 100 items at this nonprofit site developed and maintained by Toke Ward Petersen.
- *OSTEI*, Hong Kong University of Science and Technology (http://home.ust. hk/~eteval/ostei/introduction.htm). OSTEI will allow you to either choose a question from the system question bank or to create one yourself. When making a question, five types of question options are available: text box, large text box, pull-down option, radio button, and check box. This means that you can create open-ended questions as well as multiple choice questions online.
- *Quia* (http://www.quia.com/). Create quizzes and other learning activities on the Quia Web site. Also makes available already created quizzes in several subject areas. Designed for K-12 instruction. Registration required.
- *Quiz Center* (http://school.discovery.com/quizcenter/). Create, administer, and grade quizzes online. Must join My Discovery and set up a Custom Classroom.

Class management tools

Online class management refers to those tasks that are usually considered clerical or administrative in the traditional classroom. This would include student enrollments, drops, grading, student tracking, assignment scheduling, and other similar tasks. Computer systems can play a major role in eliminating some of the drudgery of these types of tasks, as well as adding some new ways of tracking students that may not have been available in traditional classrooms. Here are some questions to consider when designing or selecting a class management system (CMS):

- Do you want single-user authentication? Do you want the students to be able to enter their ID and password once and then be automatically entered into all courses for which they have enrolled?
- Do you want student interaction with Web pages tracked? Because Web pages for your course(s) reside on the server, this can be logged on the basis of user identification information.
- Do you want the capability of storing individual courses, Web pages, and objects in a database for later retrieval or sharing? This requires a database system and a method of identifying the specific elements (page, section, or object) that you wish to store and tag.
- Do you want some interface with your student registration system (automatic enrollment of students in the courses and some type of automatic acknowledgment sent to the students)?

- What type of grade book capabilities do you desire (automatic entering of grades from online quizzes and tests, manual entry of grades, student viewing)?

Most class management tools are commercial programs with varying levels of cost. Several universities have developed applications (such as WebCT) that have now become commercial offerings. One free class management tool developed for the K-12 environment is ClassBuilder, http://www.classbuilder.com/macdl.htm. The commercial tools are discussed in the "Selecting an integrated course management tool" section of this chapter.

Selecting an integrated course management tool

For those institutions that do not wish to find and manage a number of tools, or to build their own user interface, the best option is to select an integrated course management system. The increased use of the Web for teaching has led many universities and commercial providers to develop system-level support for educators. Each of these systems helps to reduce the effort and skill needed to build a Web-based course. Most of the better tools incorporate all of the features we've discussed in this chapter: information distribution, communications, assessment, and course management. Because of the complexity of these integrated tools, you need to be careful when beginning your evaluation. Sometimes a tool will appear to be an integrated tool when in fact it is a single tool that acts more as a portal. For example, First Class was designed as a course management tool. But although it allows you to link Web pages, communication programs, and assessment programs within its framework, it does not give you the integrated framework within its own software. Three steps will help you in your evaluation of the integrated systems.

1. *Review other sites* that have already completed a course tool evaluation. Many of these sites provide informative matrices of features that compare one tool with another. A sample of such review sites is below:

- Online Educational Delivery Applications Project, http://www.c2t2.ca/landonline/evalapps.asp
- FutureU, http://www.futureu.com/cmscomp/cms_comp.html
- Murdoch University, http://cleo.murdoch.edu.au/teach/guide/res/examples/course-servers.html

2. *Develop a list of your criteria* for an integrated system. Which specific capabilities will you use and what do you plan to use in the future? Some features to consider are listed below within general categories:

- System tools:
    User authentication
    Security
    Resource monitoring
    Data recovery

      Student and faculty support
      Help support
- Information distribution tools:
      Web browsing and linking
      Bookmarks
      Multimedia support
      Security
- Communication tools:
      E-mail
      Threaded discussions
      Newsgroups
      Chat
      Whiteboard
      Private and public shared spaces
      Audio and video conferencing
      Easily accessible transcripts
- Instructor tools:
      Course development
      Course planning
      Course revising
      Course monitoring
      Electronic editing
- Course assessment and management tools:
      Access analysis
      Page and/or object database capabilities
      Graded and ungraded assessment
      Automatic population from enrollments
      Add and drop capabilities
      Student progress tracking
      Prescription capabilities
      Calendaring
- Technical/administration considerations:
      Ease of installation and maintenance
      Server software
      Client software
      Scalability
      Availability of source code or ease of modification/customization

3. *Create a prototype course* that you will use to test the systems you are seriously considering. Your prototype should include several Web pages with a variety of links, a good number of students (twenty-five to fifty), and some typical activities that you want the students to do, such as posting to a discussion board, participating in a chat, and sharing a paper for peer review and critique. The content of your prototype is less important than the variety of capabilities that it demonstrates. Use your prototype to test each system for ease of use and support.

Finally, as you evaluate each tool, be sure to pay close attention to the user interface. Is it pleasing to you? Does it give the type of image you wish to portray for your institution? If not, can you customize it for your needs? How much training will be required for students and faculty to feel comfortable using this course tool? It might help to keep a journal of your reviews, because the complexity of these tools can seem overwhelming. Check with other institutions that use the tool and, if possible, pilot a course or two using the tools you select prior to making a heavy financial and training investment.

Remember, these tools can make setting up your Web instruction environment much easier. However, choose carefully! You will be committed to the tool for many years (if not decades). Once you have invested significant money, time, and training in its implementation, making a change at a later date will be very painful and costly.

7   Evaluating student mastery and program effectiveness

Evaluation of students in Web-based education should occur much as it does in traditional classroom settings. The key is determining how to do that when students are not physically present. It is equally important to evaluate the course effectiveness and the success of the entire Web-based program.

For over two decades, a dualistic debate has raged over whether assessment should focus on accountability or improvement. Today, most educators have come to accept that dealing with both is important. However, this chapter will concentrate on evaluation as being first and foremost about improving student learning and secondarily about determining accountability for the quality of learning produced.

Angelo (1999) discussed the challenges of student and program assessment. He proposed four pillars of transformative assessment to help evaluation move forward within a learning community of students and faculty involved in assessment. His four pillars are:

- *Build shared trust*. Encouraging participants to share examples of successful teaching or assessment practices allows them to present their best face and demonstrates that each is a smart person with ideas to contribute.
- *Build shared motivation*. Most people are more productive when working toward clear, personally meaningful, reasonable goals.
- *Build shared language and concepts*. Develop a collective understanding of language and new concepts (mental models) for describing, manipulating, and meeting the goals.
- *Build shared research guidelines*. Individual campuses and programs can benefit from constructing their own specific lists of principles or guidelines that serve as the criteria for evaluating their own assessment plans and efforts.

Angelo (1999) accurately summarized the purpose of assessment when he said: "If we plan and conduct our assessment projects at every step as if learning matters most – and not just student learning, but ours as well – then the distance between means and ends will be reduced and our chances for success increased."

Evaluating student mastery

Teachers have been evaluating students since formal education began. Student mastery may be assessed through a variety of methods, including oral interviews, written tests, practical application of concepts and procedures, and asking students to teach the concept or skill to someone else. Unfortunately, both in traditional education and in Web-based education, student evaluation is often given short shrift when designing instruction. Usually this misconnection in evaluation occurs because teachers or course designers fail to create a direct relationship between instructional objectives and assessment measures. To establish this connection, three key ideas are crucial:

- Obtain a good match between the type of objective you wish to measure (e.g. knowledge, skills, attitudes) and the means you use to measure it. Bloom (1956) provided a well-respected taxonomy for objectives and knowledge management.
- Use several data sources to gain as complete a picture as possible.
- Remember that not all instructional objectives lend themselves to direct, precise measurement.

Table 7.1 provides examples of typical poor measurements for types of knowledge or skills and examples of a better evaluation tactic.

In each of the instances, the teachers or course designers thought they were measuring the objective. However, in each situation the measurement was at a lower level in Bloom's taxonomy. The objectives were asking for the measurement of demonstrations, analysis, and synthesis, whereas the original measurement strategy was evaluating knowledge – particularly lower-level knowledge such as identification and recall. The final example tries to measure application through writing the program. However, the ability to construct a program does not measure the ability to analyze one that is already constructed.

Bloom's taxonomy can be used to help phrase an objective so that you and the learner know what he or she is expected to be able to do after the lesson or the course. The levels indicate whether the learning involves the learner in lower or higher-order thinking. There is no good or bad; however, you want to help students progress to the highest level they are able to achieve. Do not underestimate your students' abilities in this area. Bereiter and Scardamalia (2000) found that even young children (aged 3–12) are capable of higher-order thinking skills earlier than previously thought. Among young children age 3–10 they found clear evidence of children participating in both application and analysis. Children age 10–12 also reached the higher-order skills of analysis and synthesis, with occasional evaluation. Keeping this in mind, it seems teachers should work toward more teaching and mastery activities at these higher-order thinking skill levels both at a young age and certainly in adolescence and adulthood.

When determining how to measure mastery of these levels it is beneficial to match the expected products that measure mastery with the level of the taxonomy.

Table 7.1 Poor measurements and alternatives for better evaluation

Skill or knowledge description tactics	Typical poor measurements	Alternative measurement tactics
A course in leadership included objectives that were based in demonstrating specific skills or behaviors	Multiple choice knowledge test of terms and concepts *Instead of measuring the ability to perform skills (application on Bloom's taxonomy), this type of evaluation tactic measures only knowledge by recall*	Demonstrations of desired behaviors during a role-play Demonstration of desired skills within a real-world environment Analysis and resolution of a case study requiring use of specific skills or behaviors
An advanced French course included objectives for students to analyze historic events that influenced the current French culture	Matching a list of events to a list of influences Listing the major events that led to the French revolution Writing an essay, in French, describing a current cultural phenomenon *Although this measures a slightly higher level of knowledge, it still does not meet the objective of analysis. Instead, it measures recall and memorization*	Analyze a French story that includes historic elements and discuss what, if any, of those elements are still seen today Students provide peer critiques of current French culture based on acceptance or rejection of historical events
A computer science class includes objectives for analyzing an administrative accounting system and providing recommendations for changes	Write an accounting program that performs specific functions On a fill-in-the-blank test list seven considerations for a good accounting system *In this example, skills are being measured in terms of programming expertise, but analysis and synthesis are not. The fill-in again measures only recall*	Provide students with several case studies or sample programs to critique Ask students to evaluate the accounting system in their work environment and write an executive report of recommendations

Table 7.2 gives some examples of potential measurement products at different levels in Bloom's taxonomy.

As discussed above, the difficulty in accurately assessing student mastery lies in the accurate definition of learning objectives, as well as the teaching and assessment of those objectives. Two decades ago, English (1978) illustrated this difficulty in his discussion of the "fictional curriculum." This is the declared curriculum – what it is assumed the student is learning. However, this may differ from the "real" or

Table 7.2 Potential measurement products

Learning outcomes	Products
Know: define, memorize, recall, relate, list, label, declare, tell, describe, locate, state, find, name	Lists of main events Facts chart Acrostics Outlines Notes Databases
Comprehend: restate, paraphrase, explain, report, discuss, review, interpret, translate, predict, compare	Cut out or draw pictures to show an event Write or perform a play based on the story or sequence of events Write a summary report of an event Flow-chart the sequence of events Written/oral interpretation of research or theory
Apply: apply, generate, solve, intervene, demonstrate, use, illustrate, construct, complete, classify	Complete research with conclusions and recommendations Troubleshoot a project Construct a model to demonstrate how it will work Make a diorama to illustrate an important event Write a journal or make a scrapbook about the areas of study Design a market strategy for your product using a known strategy as a model Write a paper/textbook about the topic for others to use Present the topic and answer questions
Analyze: distinguish, question, analyze, dissect, inspect, examine, categorize, classify, compare and contrast, investigate, separate	Written/oral case study Categorize different concepts Design a questionnaire to gather information Write a commercial to sell a new product Flow chart the critical stages Build a concept map to show relationships Write a biography of the study person Review a work of art in terms of form, color, and texture
Synthesize: compose, propose, design, create, construct, predict, propose, devise, formulate, imagine	Case study solution Written/oral recommendations for problem-solving Written/oral research design Written/oral program or strategic plan Invent a machine to do a specific task Create a new product Write/talk about your feelings in relation to the topic Write a television show, play, puppet show,

role play, song or pantomime about the
topic
Make up a new language code and write
material using it
Sell an idea
Compose a rhythm or put new words to a
known melody
Defend a client in a mock trial

Evaluate: judge, evaluate, compare, contrast, value, choose, rate, assess, measure, defend, justify, critique, argue, recommend, prioritize, determine	Debates Symposiums Forums Position papers Written/oral defense Diagnose a patient Prepare a list of criteria to judge an event Make a booklet about ten rules you consider important Write a letter to your boss advising on changes needed in the organization Act as judge or jury in a mock trial

taught curriculum – that is, the curriculum as it is delivered to the student. It may also differ from the "tested" curriculum – what students actually learn. Finding tools to help in keeping the links between learning, teaching, and assessment is key to student success and to accurate measurement.

Eanes (2001) provided another ingenious tool to be used in the first step of writing accurate objectives and linking them to products. This tool is the Task-oriented Construction Wheel, based on Bloom's taxonomy. The wheel, shown in Figure 7.1, categorizes the taxonomy into four quarters that allow movement between the cognitive levels:

- Information-gathering – knowledge and comprehension.
- Making use of knowledge – comprehension and application.
- Taking apart – analysis and synthesis.
- Judging the outcome – synthesis and evaluation.

The wheel places the six parts of Bloom's cognitive levels in the center. The spokes of the wheel radiate outward to include active verbs to be used in writing the objectives relating to those cognitive levels. The outside radius presents the potential products for measuring those cognitive levels.

Another tool to use when planning any instructional design is to create a matrix to link outcomes, strategies and assessment. By placing your lessons into the matrix you help to ensure that there is a direct relationship between your learning objectives and your teaching strategies. You can also easily determine whether you are, in fact, assessing each learning objective. If you find you are not teaching or assessing an outcome, then you need to evaluate what to do. Is the outcome important? If so, add an additional teaching strategy and assessment. If not, delete the outcome from

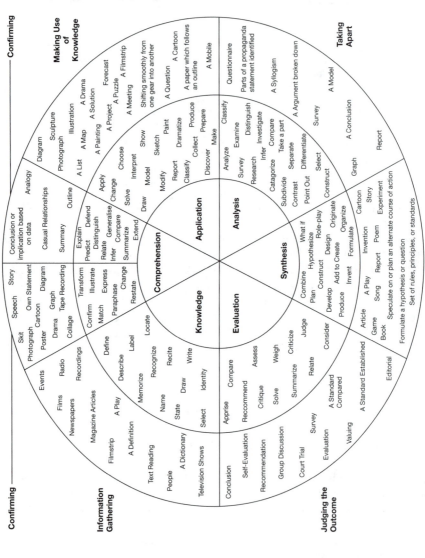

Figure 7.1 Task-oriented question construction wheel based on Bloom's taxonomy. From Eanes (2001), copyright © 2001 St Edward's University Center for Teaching Excellence, by permission

your list. It is possible to combine several objectives/outcomes under one teaching strategy or one assessment tool. Table 7.3 is an example of two lessons, from an online business communications course, placed in the matrix.

Note that the matrix uses student assessments other than typical objective testing. This is due to learning outcomes that require more than the lower-order thinking skills of knowledge and comprehension. Also note that in each case the assessment tool or instrument measures more than one objective at a time. This helps to lessen the teacher work load for separate discrete measurement of each objective.

Another key factor in both of the examples in the matrix is the use of collaboration and the social construction of knowledge. Encouraging more cooperation and networking among peers has become important to many teachers today, and the Internet makes this possible. However, some instructors find difficulty in evaluating networking and collaboration in the Web-based environment. Networked projects are often dynamic, active, and constantly changing. They incorporate various activities by participants in different locations reacting or sharing at different times.

Ravitz (1997) and Reigeluth (1995) discuss the shift that takes place as education moves toward an information-sharing paradigm. This conversational learning method sometimes frightens educators new to the Web, as they feel a "loss of control" over the content and must deal with an added layer of complexity not usually encountered in the more controlled environment of a traditional lecture and test class.

Five examples of translating these assessment techniques to the online environment are discussed here: giving up control, reassessing outcome evaluation beyond testing, real-world application, project-based learning assessment, and student reflection as assessment.

Giving up control

One of the most difficult aspects of teaching online is the inability to see the students. Teachers rely on "controlling" the classroom environment and thus controlling and evaluating student outcomes. For example, in a speech class the course objective is usually for the student to be able to make effective, persuasive presentations. The unstated outcome is probably that the student will be able to do this even after leaving the class. The usual measurement of this objective relies on having the student give an oral presentation to the class. The instructor then evaluates the student's presentation based on several criteria such as articulation, presence, body language, ability to answer questions, and audience control. The teacher may also ask the class to provide some peer critique of the speech. How then can this same evaluation and subsequent learning occur in an online course?

The first step is giving control of the student's assessment to the student instead of to the instructor. This takes a great deal of trust of both yourself and the design of the course, as well as faith in the student's ability to learn from assessment outside of your purview. First, you must believe that the online course has already presented the knowledge base needed for the student to be an effective presenter (e.g. information about how to stand, how to speak, how to gauge the audience). Second, you must provide students with an opportunity to test that knowledge. This might

Table 7.3 Teaching strategies

Lesson description	Lesson-specific learning objectives	Teaching strategies	Outcomes assessment
Introduction to successful organization communication *Reading assignment: Chapters 1–2*	1 Describe how managers use communication 2 Contrast the formal and informal communication channels within the organization 3 Analyze the differences between internal and external communication networks 4 Discuss factors that contribute to effective business communication 5 Develop goals for acquiring communication skills the student will need in their career 6 Describe the use of verbal vs. nonverbal communication 7 Identify the steps in the communication process 8 Summarize what can be done to improve communication	1 Diagram of formal and informal communication 2 Video examples of effective and ineffective communication 3 Demonstration of nonverbal communication 4 Discussion of student experiences with business communication	Students will write a reflective essay in which they reflect on their work context and describe the type of communication that occurs, their part in it, and how it can be improved. They must include a summarized plan for improvement that includes the student's participation as a leader or "example-setter"
Intercultural communication *Reading assignment: Chapter 3*	1 Discuss trends that have made intercultural business communication so important	1 Post five case study examples of intercultural business communication difficulties	Participate in a bulletin board discussion regarding this topic. Specific questions will be posed to generate the outcomes needed based on the teaching strategies.

2 Discuss ways people can differ culturally and skills that will assist in communication 3 Research a particular culture and its differing communication 4 Identify the common misunderstandings in written and inter-cultural communication	2 Ask students to evaluate the communication in terms of their reading and to respond with possible solutions.	Students will also be required to share their research by posting the URLs to the bulletin board.

be done by having students do a presentation for a group, of their choice, in their home location (e.g. a local school, a civic organization, a church, their place of business, etc.). Give the students an evaluation criteria sheet – the same rubric you would use to evaluate the students in class – and ask them to have one or more audience members complete the evaluation following the speech. Finally, ask the student to use those evaluations to reflect on the speech and discuss what went well, what could be improved, and to rework the presentation for another iteration.

In giving up control of the evaluation, several things occurred in this example:

- The student is given responsibility for learning and for evaluation.
- The student learns to use resources outside of the teacher for ongoing assessment beyond the course.
- The evaluation reflects a real-world environment instead of that in the classroom.
- The student must use the higher-order thinking skills of application, analysis, synthesis, and evaluation in writing a reflection of the event.

In keeping with the tradition of "doing assessment as if learning matters most," it seems that this type of assessment provides accurate reflection of the learning objective and best assists the student.

Reassessing outcome evaluation: beyond objective testing

One of the unfortunate developments of Web-based education has been the increasing use of "objective" testing (i.e. multiple choice, true/false, fill-in-the-blank, etc.). Because of the speed of testing and feedback, it is a natural use of the online environment. Certainly, there is a place for this type of mastery testing – that is, when assessing lower-order thinking skills such as knowledge or comprehension. Writing objective test questions that also measure higher-order thinking skills effectively is very difficult (and therefore this method is rarely used).

Furthermore, by relying solely on episodic objective testing (e.g. a mid-term and a final) of student mastery you exclude several groups of skilled students: those who do not do well with this type of testing, those who learn over time, and those who learn best through actual experience. Learning is a complex process. It entails not only what students know but what they can do with that knowledge. Also, it goes beyond knowledge to values, attitudes, and performance beyond the classroom. Thus your assessment of student mastery should include a diverse array of methods.

A survey of US colleges and universities found that methods of assessing students continue to be traditional, emphasizing quantitative instruments. Institutions do make limited use of more innovative – and usually more qualitative – assessment techniques such as portfolios, capstone projects, and observations of student performance. However, only 34 percent indicated they engaged in more complex assessment activities, such as collecting information about higher-order thinking skills, affective development, or professional skills. Even fewer (23 percent) asked students about their civic or social activities. Is it enough to rely on the easily quantifiable indicators of student mastery in the name of consistency? Or should we risk some inconsistency and seek to effectively measure mastery that will matter in the student's transition from school to the real world?

Real-world application

A mantra of constructivism theory has been *situated cognition* – the concept that students will learn more if the theory is presented in relation to real-world applications. This makes the learning relevant to the student's situation. The Web-based learning environment provides a unique opportunity to capitalize on this situated cognition approach to learning. As pointed out previously, you are already in a position of giving up control when teaching in the Web-based environment. One effective way to both give up control and provide a real-world learning experience is to require students to apply the new knowledge in their own environments.

For example, an online education graduate program at a Florida university requires that most homework assignments be applied in the real world. In the doctoral research class, instead of working statistical problems with case studies or common book examples, students are required to actually administer a survey in their work environments, gather and analyze the data, and write a report as their culminating assignment.

An undergraduate organizational communications course at an Ohio university requires students to analyze communications in their workplace for one of the assignments, then make recommendations for improvement. A fourth grade elementary school in Georgia requires students to demonstrate examples of physics that they experience in their own homes. All of these examples use situated cognition to teach, reinforce, and assess complex concepts.

Having students apply their learning to real-world situations demonstrates the use of several higher-order thinking skills: application, analysis, and synthesis. It also helps to meet the often unarticulated outcome of continuing to use the concepts even after leaving the course.

Project-based learning evaluation

Similar to real-world application of concepts, project-based learning provides analogous benefits. The examples of real-world evaluation given in the topic above are also examples of project-based learning. In each of those situations, the student is presented with a problem to analyze and resolve through making recommendations. This type of project-based learning evaluation requires synthesis of many concepts as well as evaluation and prioritizing of the concepts when selecting on which to report.

In addition to having students demonstrate mastery of skills and knowledge, project-based learning can also allow the teacher to assess the scaffolding of concepts. A complex project can be built that requires the student to follow a procedure in order to complete it. Then the teacher can evaluate where in the procedure problems may occur. Another type of project-based scaffolding evaluation would occur in a topic that requires prior knowledge to succeed. For example, a project that requires doing a trial balance in accounts would also require the student to know how to extract information correctly from credit and debit journal items. The combination of a procedure and prior knowledge and understanding may be followed to see where in the learning the student may have difficulties.

Another type of scaffolding evaluation would be for conceptual development that is based on relationships that are not necessarily linear. For example, in an undergraduate business ethics course an instructor assigned a project of creating a collage of pictures and words that represented the ethics concepts covered in the course. This type of project has the potential of revealing much more than a simple definition of ethics or any absolute reflection of right and wrong. The collage may reveal several levels of ethical dilemmas, a pictorial representation of affective domains relating to ethics, as well as a philosophy about ethics. The project requires multiple inputs and outputs to meet the assignment and thus accurately reflected the inherent individuality in ethics and values. Here evaluating student mastery through a project probably netted much more information than the traditional multiple choice test or short essay.

The use of student reflection papers

Chinese philosophy teaches us about *yin* and *yang*. Too often, in the daily lives of many westerners as well as in our approach to education, we concentrate only on the *yang* – the doing, the demonstrating, the creating. In fact, many educators completely ignore the *yin* – the reflection, the patient waiting, the quiet times. However, for many students, taking time for reflection (*yin*) is the best way for them to internalize knowledge and thus to retain it past the end of the course.

Teachers often mistakenly believe that there is no need to give time for reflection, as the students who need it will find a means to do so on their own. Instead these instructors concentrate on how to pour more information into the perceived empty vessel of student minds. Unfortunately, this method is usually not successful. In the first place, students are not empty vessels awaiting the teacher's knowledge. Rather, student minds are like ours, filled with all types of important information, special needs, and many distractions. Students, like the rest of us, also have busy lives filled with *yang* and therefore they parse their time to meet only the immediate needs of learning at the moment. Even if they yearn for some reflective time, like us students find it is hard to schedule reflection into their daily lives.

The assignment of reflection papers does two important things. (1) It allows (forces) students to take time to reflect on their learning. (2) It provides the instructor with invaluable information about the students' perceptions of the topic, the development of potential innovative concepts or uses based on their learning, and highlights any misconceptions. When required to engage in reflection during a course, students' end-of-course evaluations often include comments such as "I didn't realize how much I learned until I did this assignment," or "I learned so much more in this course because I was forced to take time and think about how it affected me."

Using reflection papers for evaluation can come in several forms:

- *Journals*. Students chronicle their perceptions of learning, topic relevance, and applications throughout a course
- *Specific reflection papers*. Students ponder a specific concept, dilemma, case study, and write descriptions of their feelings as they work through the assignment.
- *Beginning-of-course reflections*. Students usually note their preconceived expectations of the course, the teacher, the content, their fears or interests in relation to the topic.
- *End-of-course reflections*. Students evaluate the impact of the course in their learning or their lives.
- *Debriefing reflections*. Students take a short period of time to record what went well or what went wrong following a specific learning event (e.g. a presentation, a role-play situation, a group project).

If we are truly using evaluation to make learning matter, the use of reflection is a key ingredient in the complexity of student mastery.

Finally, to summarize student assessment, let us look at the American Association for Higher Education's nine principles of good practice for assessing student learning (used with permission):

1   *The assessment of student learning begins with educational values.* Assessment is not an end in itself but a vehicle for educational improvement. Its effective practice, then, begins with and enacts a vision of the kinds of learning we most value for students and strive to help them achieve. Educational values should drive not only *what* we choose to assess but also *how* we do so. Where questions about educational mission and values are skipped over, assessment threatens to be an exercise in measuring what's easy, rather than a process of improving what we really care about.

2   *Assessment is most effective when it reflects an understanding of learning as multidimensional, integrated, and revealed in performance over time.*

Learning is a complex process. It entails not only what students know but what they can do with what they know; it involves not only knowledge and abilities but values, attitudes, and habits of mind that affect both academic success and performance beyond the classroom. Assessment should reflect these understandings by employing a diverse array of methods, including those that call for actual performance, using them over time so as to reveal change, growth, and increasing degrees of integration. Such an approach aims for a more complete and accurate picture of learning, and therefore firmer bases for improving our students' educational experience.

3   *Assessment works best when the programs it seeks to improve have clear, explicitly stated purposes.* Assessment is a goal-oriented process. It entails comparing educational performance with educational purposes and expectations – those derived from the institution's mission, from faculty intentions in program and course design, and from knowledge of students' own goals. Where program purposes lack specificity or agreement, assessment as a process pushes a campus toward clarity about where to aim and what standards to apply; assessment also prompts attention to where and how program goals will be taught and learned. Clear, shared, implementable goals are the cornerstone for assessment that is focused and useful.

4   *Assessment requires attention to outcomes but also and equally to the experiences that lead to those outcomes.* Information about outcomes is of high importance; where students "end up" matters greatly. But to improve outcomes, we need to know about student experience along the way – about the curricula, teaching, and kind of student effort that lead to particular outcomes. Assessment can help us understand which students learn best under what conditions; with such knowledge comes the capacity to improve the whole of their learning.

5   *Assessment works best when it is ongoing not episodic.* Assessment is a process whose power is cumulative. Though isolated, "one-shot" assessment can be better than none, improvement is best fostered when assessment entails a linked series of activities undertaken over time. This may mean tracking the process of individual students, or of cohorts of students; it may mean collecting the same examples of student performance or using the same instrument semester after semester. The point is to monitor progress toward intended goals in a spirit of continuous improvement. Along the way, the assessment process itself should be evaluated and refined in light of emerging insights.

6   *Assessment fosters wider improvement when representatives from across the educational community are involved.* Student learning is a campus-wide responsibility, and assessment is a way of enacting that responsibility. Thus, while assessment efforts may start small, the aim over time is to involve people from across the educational community. Faculty play an especially important role, but assessment's questions can't be fully addressed without participation by student-affairs educators, librarians,

administrators, and students. Assessment may also involve individuals from beyond the campus (alumni/ae, trustees, employers) whose experience can enrich the sense of appropriate aims and standards for learning. Thus understood, assessment is not a task for small groups of experts but a collaborative activity; its aim is wider, better-informed attention to student learning by all parties with a stake in its improvement.

7   *Assessment makes a difference when it begins with issues of use and illuminates questions that people really care about.* Assessment recognizes the value of information in the process of improvement. But to be useful, information must be connected to issues or questions that people really care about. This implies assessment approaches that produce evidence that relevant parties will find credible, suggestive, and applicable to decisions that need to be made. It means thinking in advance about how the information will be used, and by whom. The point of assessment is not to gather data and return "results"; it is a process that starts with the questions of decision-makers, that involves them in the gathering and interpreting of data, and that informs and helps guide continuous improvement.

8   *Assessment is most likely to lead to improvement when it is part of a larger set of conditions that promote change.* Assessment alone changes little. Its greatest contribution comes on campuses where the quality of teaching and learning is visibly valued and worked at. On such campuses, the push to improve educational performance is a visible and primary goal of leadership; improving the quality of undergraduate education is central to the institution's planning, budgeting, and personnel decisions. On such campuses, information about learning outcomes is seen as an integral part of decision making, and avidly sought.

9   *Through assessment, educators meet responsibilities to students and to the public.* There is a compelling public stake in education. As educators, we have a responsibility to the publics that support or depend on us to provide information about the ways in which our students meet goals and expectations. But that responsibility goes beyond the reporting of such information; our deeper obligation – to ourselves, our students, and society – is to improve. Those to whom educators are accountable have a corresponding obligation to support such attempts at improvement.

Program evaluation

With the surge in public demand for accountability and some concern over the viability of Web-based learning in terms of quality, it is important to have a good program evaluation in place. However, beyond the needs of political justification, it is essential that your program evaluation accurately informs changes in curriculum, teaching strategies, and student assessment.

Recognizing that good programs are made that way through constant vigilance and by learning from feedback received along the way, you will be faced with several preliminary decisions:

- What decisions do you want to make as a result of the evaluation?
- Are you interested primarily in program improvement or in justifying the existence, removal, or expansion of a program?
- Do you want to use an inside or outside evaluator?
- Do you want to use a quantitative or qualitative evaluation strategy?

Determining an evaluation strategy will be essential in fulfilling whatever your mission is for evaluation, or in answering the questions you have posed. For example, a quantitative strategy might look at factors such as numbers of enrollees, their ratings of program quality, the percentage of graduates, perceptions of persons dropping out or graduation from the program. A quantitative strategy might be most useful in taking program action such as expanding course offerings or adding a new degree program. A qualitative approach might examine profiles of students based on regional location qualities, how studying takes place, how leadership is exerted, how grades are obtained, and how resources (such as libraries and Internet access) outside of the university are used. A qualitative strategy is used to understand the learning process, what is going on, and how it might be influenced from within or from outside to provide a more satisfying educational experience.

Web-based program evaluation is usually divided into two areas: content and instructor evaluation. Certainly, it is difficult to separate the two elements, as they are inextricably linked. However, for this chapter we will examine the necessity of evaluating these two areas separately and provide some sample student survey tools that may assist you in gathering some data.

Content evaluation

Researchers often complain that one of the biggest weaknesses in the design and development of Web-based education programs is failure to routinely assess the effectiveness of the materials and media. Evaluation should be practiced continuously through the design, development, and implementation cycles to ensure that things work as anticipated and intended.

Moore and Kearsley (1996) identified two key criteria of content delivery evaluation: data collection methods and measures. Table 7.4 looks at these two categories and describes methods that can be used to evaluate Web-based instruction. Each technique has strengths and weaknesses. To get the best results it is recommended that more than one technique and several measures be used to obtain a complete picture of how well a course or program is working. Evaluation experts also recommend that a neutral party should conduct the evaluation – that is, someone who is not part of the course or program design team.

Moore and Kearsley (1996) identified twelve general principles to consider when evaluating any course design:

- *Good structure.* Course materials must be well defined and display internal consistency among different parts of the course.
- *Clear objectives.* Identify suitable learning experiences and subsequent evaluation.

Table 7.4 Evaluating Web-based instruction

Methods	Measures
Student observations through online monitoring	Chat transcripts Bulletin board postings Teleconference recording Web page access records Course element use Response analysis of testing
Questionnaires and interviews	What problems are students experiencing? Protocol analysis (think aloud while learning) In-text questionnaire (reactions to material requested as the student works through it) Student satisfaction surveys
Course prototyping for formative evaluation prior to course being offered	Small test group for design ideas Individual testing with selected pilot students or groups
Focus group	Group discusses or reacts to course ideas Group is asked to answer specific questions about course functionality

- *Small unit*. The content and course organization should be presented in small units, preferably that correspond to a single instructional objective or learning activity.
- *Planned participation*. Opportunities for student interaction should be embedded throughout the course materials.
- *Completeness*. Extensive commentary or examples should be provided.
- *Repetition*. Important ideas are reinforced to compensate for distractions and memory limitations.
- *Synthesis*. Important ideas are woven together (usually in summaries).
- *Stimulation*. Materials capture and hold the attention of students through varied formats, content, or guest participation.
- *Variety*. Format and media variety are present to appeal to student interests, backgrounds, and learning styles.
- *Open-ended*. Assignments, examples, and problems allow students to adapt the content to their own situations.
- *Feedback*. Regular feedback is provided on assignments and student progress in the course.
- *Continual evaluation*. The effectiveness of materials, media, and instructional strategies are routinely assessed using a variety of methods.

The use of student surveys is one method of gathering summative data for evaluation. When developing this type of tool, however, it is important to ensure the students understand the separation of the course content (materials, assignments, activities) from the instructor's participation, personality, or additions. It is also important to determine, in advance, what aspects of the course delivery are important or desired. In other words you need to have a concept of what constitutes a "good" course before attempting to develop an effective evaluation instrument. Does your concept include the use of images, specific interaction requirements, or a variety of learning styles? Whatever you determine is consistently important from one course to the next should be included in your survey instrument. One example of an online course evaluation instrument used successfully is presented below.

Online Course Evaluation

The University wishes to ensure continued effective, high quality curriculum. Your input into your experience of this course is very important. All evaluations are submitted anonymously. The instructor will not receive the evaluations until after completion of the term and all grades are mailed. The evaluation results will be compiled, maintaining your anonymity, then presented to the instructor and course developers for improving the course.

Please respond by clicking the number which best matches your opinion on a scale of 0 to 5, where 0 indicates you strongly disagree with the statement, and 5 means you strongly agree with the statement. There is also space for comments at the end of the form.

1	I was able to navigate the course Web pages with ease.	0 1 2 3 4 5
2	My first impression of the course was positive.	0 1 2 3 4 5
3	The identity of the University and the instructor(s) was readily evident.	0 1 2 3 4 5
4	The Web links were relevant and interesting.	0 1 2 3 4 5
5	I was able to view each part of the course in any order.	0 1 2 3 4 5
6	I was required to use several resources (e.g. Web links, textbook(s), chat, bulletin board) to construct knowledge.	0 1 2 3 4 5
7	I was able to interact with my instructor effectively.	0 1 2 3 4 5
8	I was able to interact with my classmates effectively.	0 1 2 3 4 5
9	I was able to post results of my work in a shared space (e.g. bulletin board, Web pages).	0 1 2 3 4 5
10	I was encouraged to use my own initiative to find relevant and timely information pertinent to my studies.	0 1 2 3 4 5
11	The assignments were interesting and relevant to the course and the "real world".	0 1 2 3 4 5

12	The combination of text, graphics, and interaction in the course was appropriate and enhanced my learning.	0 1 2 3 4 5
13	The course was educational.	0 1 2 3 4 5
14	The course was intellectually challenging.	0 1 2 3 4 5
15	I would recommend this course to others.	0 1 2 3 4 5

Comments:

Instructor evaluation

For the individual teacher conducting a Web-based course, the indicators of how the class is going are in many ways similar to on-campus instruction. Some sources of information to help shape and maintain quality in a course are:

* E-mail messages from students.
* Student verbal or written feedback about the class in reflection assignments.
* Student debriefing comments or sentiments, favorable or unfavorable, following specific activities.
* End-of-course instructor evaluations.

A sticky subject at most schools is the evaluation of the instructor. In the university system, end-of-course student evaluations often serve for promotion and tenure purposes. Consequently the creation, validating, and reliability of any instruments used for this purpose is of high concern to faculty.

As with the course evaluation, it is important to identify in advance what aspects of online course facilitation are considered key success factors. For example, is it important for the instructor to be in regular contact with the students? Is the instructor expected to develop, on the fly, additional Web-based materials as students need them? How much interaction outside of e-mail (e.g. chat room participation, bulletin board posting, specific electronic comments on homework, etc.) is expected of a good instructor? How much of the instructor's enthusiasm for the topic is expected? All of these and many more aspects of Web-based course delivery need to be weighed and prioritized prior to developing an instrument.

The sample instructor evaluation instrument below is one that has been used successfully.

Online instructor evaluation

The University wishes to ensure continued effective, high quality instruction. Your input into your experience with your instructor is very important. All evaluations are submitted anonymously. The instructor will not receive the evaluations until after completion of the term and all grades are mailed. The results will be compiled, maintaining your anonymity, then presented to the instructor.

   Please respond by clicking the number which best matches your opinion on a scale of 0 to 5, where 0 indicates you strongly disagree with the statement, and 5 means you strongly agree with the statement. There is also space for comments at the end of the form.

1	The instructor used effective teaching methods.	0 1 2 3 4 5
2	The instructor was well prepared for the class.	0 1 2 3 4 5
3	The instructor maintained a high level of academic standards.	0 1 2 3 4 5
4	The instructor provided opportunities to develop my communication skills.	0 1 2 3 4 5
5	The instructor provided opportunities for collaboration.	0 1 2 3 4 5
6	The instructor provided opportunities to develop my active research skills.	0 1 2 3 4 5
7	The instructor provided opportunities to develop my critical-thinking skills.	0 1 2 3 4 5
8	The instructor provided real-world problems to solve which were relevant to the course.	0 1 2 3 4 5
9	The instructor provided opportunities to develop my leadership skills.	0 1 2 3 4 5
10	The instructor responded effectively to my questions and ideas.	0 1 2 3 4 5
11	The instructor demonstrated knowledge of the subject matter.	0 1 2 3 4 5
12	The instructor stimulated interest and thought.	0 1 2 3 4 5
13	The instructor was accessible to students by e-mail, phone, and in person (if the student came to campus).	0 1 2 3 4 5
14	The instructor provided feedback on assignments within the required one-week time period.	0 1 2 3 4 5
15	The instructor's strengths are:	

16   The instructor needs improvement in the following area(s):

In summary, evaluators of Web-based instruction have an opportunity to explore educational applications using a new and evolving medium. This work requires the consideration of appropriate research methods and assessment strategies. As with any evaluation design it is important to establish outcomes for the evaluation. These outcomes will then determine what constitutes student mastery, content excellence, or instructor effectiveness.

8 Miscellaneous important details

This final chapter touches on several issues that educators face in today's Web-based learning environment: copyright, intellectual property policies, keeping up with technology, accreditation of online learning, and how future trends may affect your strategic planning for online education offerings. Each of these topics is complex and could easily expand into an entire chapter or book on its own. So, rather than cover each topic in depth, this chapter will provide several Web resources where you can further research the topics if you so desire. The intent here is to point out current developments and controversy, leaving you to form the policies and procedures that best meet your organizational needs.

Copyright and the Internet

There are a number of international agreements that provide copyright protection across national borders. The major ones are the Berne Convention, the Rome Convention and TRIPs (trade-related intellectual property) agreement. The Berne Convention of 1976 changed previous copyright law to make all works immediately copyrighted upon their creation. This meant that authors, musicians, and other artists legally held copyright to their materials once it was put in any permanent form. It is no longer required to register the copyright or even to put a copyright symbol on the item – though registration and placing the symbol on works does increase the chance of success in a lawsuit. Over 170 countries agreed to this treaty and it has been the foundation of subsequent conventions.

From the perspective of Web-based education courses it is certainly wise to place the copyright symbol and a statement with each course. Some organizations elect to put the copyright statement at the bottom of every Web page. Others simply place a generic statement at the beginning of each course. Though it is not required for the protection of the work, it is a reminder to potential plagiarists that the work is not to be used without following the rules of copyright.

In the past three decades, nearly 200 countries have participated in subsequent discussions and agreements around international copyright protection. The global nature of online communication networks, the growth of digital content production technologies, and the convergence of the Internet have created an increasing need for nations to keep international copyright arrangements up to date and to continue to address each new technology. The cases involving Napster (digital music sharing) demonstrate the complexity of the issues in the digital age.

Some of the difficult legal issues framing copyright debates in the Internet age are:

- Web browsers have the ability to copy to disk and to computer memory all items encountered; this includes pages, papers, courses, etc. Is this "copying" infringing copyright?
- Is a click on a link that causes a Web server to send a page to someone else considered "publishing"?
- What rights do individuals have over their own images, voices, actions (e.g. security cameras or Web cameras that might transmit this information)?
- If your course links with information on another site and displays it within the "frame" of your course, is that infringing on copyright? Does the user believe that anything within the frame belongs to the course author?

These are just a few of the multifaceted issues facing educational institutions today. It is wise to research these issues and devise specific policies regarding their use. Many organizations have policies in place that allow the continued creation of courses with links but require a clear indication that the copyright belongs to the linked parties. For example, when the student activates an external link, it must not be displayed within the course frame. That may be accomplished by opening a new browser window or by sending the viewer away from the course altogether in order to access the linked site. Both solutions help clarify that the linked site belongs to the copyright holder.

The World Intellectual Property Organization (WIPO) has been a major force in sponsoring conventions and discussions on copyright and intellectual property. In response to new economic, social, cultural and technological developments, two new treaties on copyright were agreed at a WIPO conference in Geneva in 1996. The two treaties supplement the Berne and Rome conventions by introducing new provisions and clarifying the interpretation of existing provisions in response to the changing circumstances of world telecommunications. WIPO provides an extensive resource site of their work and the treaties at http://www.ompi.org/.

The two new treaties encompass issues specifically raised by digital and online technologies, including confirming that Article 9 of the Berne Convention, the reproduction right (copyright owners control the reproduction of the works in which they have copyright), applies in the digital environment. Additions to the Berne Convention provided various communication rights for radio and television broadcast of dramatic and musical works and for the public performance of literary and artistic works. Article 8 of Treaty 1 does not change any of the existing rights under the Berne Convention; however, an important result of the 1996 conference is an expanded *right of communication to the public* contained in Article 8. This provision clarifies and extends the scope of the Berne Convention in the light of technological change. It provides authors of literary or artistic works the right to authorize communication of their works by means of on-demand services, such as Internet availability. It will be illegal for individuals to electronically distribute copies of a computer software program or music CDs to large numbers of people without the permission of the copyright owner.

Also related to the digital agenda was a proposal (defeated after much debate) to modify the right of reproduction to explicitly include both permanent and temporary reproductions. This is an important issue because temporary reproductions are common in the use of digital information (e.g. in a computer's random access memory, or in the cache of an Internet service provider).

Article 6 of Treaty 1 (which is the right of distribution) upheld that authors of literary and artistic works shall have exclusive right to authorize public availability of the origin and copies of their works through sale or transfer of ownership. Treaty 1 also requires that contracting parties shall provide legal protection against the circumvention of effective technological measures used by authors to protect their rights (Article 11) and against removing or altering information that identifies the copyright terms and conditions (Article 12).

Following the 1996 convention, several countries crafted their own copyright Acts that encompassed many of the digital issues raised at the convention. For example, the United States began work on the Digital Millennium Copyright Act (DMCA), which was signed into law in 1998. The full Act can be viewed at http://www.lib.berkeley.edu/LAUC/copyright.html. The DMCA originally began as an outgrowth of lobbying by content providers (e.g. book publishers, software producers, video producers), who feared the Internet and digital networks would further weaken their rights, including those of fair use. Librarians and educators became aware of these efforts and fought to be a part of structuring the guide-lines, as they believed the initial suggested rules were drawn too narrowly. The guidelines were redeveloped in a national committee and they became law in 1998. However, the DMCA contains very complex and confusing language. The need to clarify the user-oriented aspects of the legislation continues to be a critical topic of debate.

A 1999 national satellite conference on continuing DMCA issues best illustrates several key points that have particular significance to Web-based education delivery. These discussions are summarized below.

- *Information policy needed.* Sharon Hogan (University Librarian, University of Illinois at Chicago) discussed the process of creating an information policy to deal with the DMCA, both to respond and comply with the Act and to build shared values within the academic institution. These policies will certainly assist in the creation of Web-based courses. She suggested having a forum for discussion that would bring together campus groups from all levels affected by the new legislation (e.g. faculty, librarians, lawyers, technological staff, museum staff, university press and printing departments, duplicating services, etc.). In fact, the DMCA requires institutions to educate their faculty, students, and staff, in order to take advantage of the higher education exemptions. She stressed the importance of including the library's mission statement, focusing on the benefits of DMCA and providing a list of resources and contacts.

- *Conduit activities and long-term storage of information.* Georgia Harper (Office of General Counsel, University of Texas) commented on the definition of "service provider" in the DMCA. It is very broad, and thus open to a variety of interpretations. Other areas of complex language apply to conduit activities (transmitting and routing material) and long-term storage of information. Examples of areas of ambiguity include links on Web pages and attachments to e-mail (e.g. a journal article). She stressed that complying with the DMCA will involve more than one person and department in the library. She also discussed the concern that the stricter laws will have a "chilling effect" on academic research.
- *Term extensions.* Laura Gasaway (Director of the Law Library and Professor of Law, University of North Carolina) discussed the Sonny Bono Copyright Term Extension Act of 1998. This Act changed the number of years before protected information moves into the public domain. Previously the rule was fifty years following the author's death. The new rule is seventy years following the author's death. Thus works that would have become public domain (not requiring permission to use) in 1998 do not have that status until 2019. This has several implications for libraries and other research endeavors. Furthermore, for corporate, anonymous and pseudonymous works the terms were extended to ninety-five years after first publication, or 120 years after creation, whichever comes first.
- *Notice of copyright requirements.* A second area discussed by Gasaway was the "notice of copyright" changes in the DMCA. Previously, libraries were simply required to provide a "notice of copyright" whenever materials were copied. This was frequently done with a stamp stating "Notice: this material might be protected by copyright." The new legislation requires libraries to reproduce the original document copyright notice. The only time libraries can use the stamp is when the copyright notice was not included on the work by the copyright holder. This change will affect procedures in interlibrary loan and copy service departments. There are also changes in the law regarding other formats, such as phonograph records and digital formats (even those used for preservation).
- *Anti-circumvention of copyrights.* The anti-circumvention aspects of DMCA deal with the technological controls that are set to prevent illegal access to online databases. Like other aspects of the DMCA, the language is very broad and open to a wide range of interpretations. As discussed by Fred Weingarten (Director of the Office of Information Technology Policy, American Library Association), since there are criminal sanctions attached to violations of this section, educators and administrators have reason to be concerned. For example, the parts of the law governing computer hardware and software could be associated with the product on your computer, on the provider's computer, at an intermediary (e.g. an internet service provider's host computer), or any combination of the above. The law states one may not "circumvent" technological control measures.
- *Copyright management information.* Weingarten also pointed out a complication regarding the section that deals with copyright management information (CMI). The law states one may not remove or alter CMI, or knowingly

distribute materials in which CMI has been removed. The concern is that sometimes the technology transmitting the information will alter text automatically. This happens with compression routines or a variety of file transfer protocols. Frequently, both the sender and the recipient are unaware anything has been altered.

In summary, copyright laws need to be carefully reviewed and policies created for each institution. It is important to designate a central resource to handle copyright questions and to maintain files of permission clearances and potential problems. Only in providing this type of resource will institutions create some security in maintaining the law. Steps to undertake in developing and maintaining your copyright policies include:

* Create policies through consultation with all affected members of the educational community.
* Provide staffing for new functions relating to compliance with policies and standards.
* Educate all institutional members around "fair use" and compliance with organizational policies. (In fact, DMCA requires the institution to educate its members on these issues.)
* Continue advocacy efforts with your country, with WIPO, and other organizations around the unfinished work, particularly as it pertains to distance education and database protection issues.

Additional information about specific issues generated by the DMCA legislation can be found at:

* www.educause.edu/issues/dmca.html
* http://www.ala.org/oitp/copyr/index.html
* http://www.aallnet.org/prodev/event_millenium.asp
* http://www.arl.org/dmca/video.html

Intellectual property policies and faculty issues

The copyright issues described above have caused a host of faculty outcries regarding intellectual property rights at many colleges and universities. Some are in the form of protests against policies of "work for hire" in the development of Web-based courses, and others are expressions of faculty fears and confusion when policies are not developed or clearly stated at their institutions. As educators and administrators struggle with articulating what belongs to the institution and what is owned by faculty who participate in the creation of online courses, teachers' unions, attorneys, faculty and staff have been striving to increase their influence in the policy development process.

At stake is the belief that the creation of Web-based courses may provide a revenue stream for the copyright holder. Whether reality and the marketplace will bear this out has yet to be seen. However, the question still remains, "Who owns a Web-based course?" Do digital courses fall under the same policies as the notes and lecture information traditionally provided by instructors in their classes? Do digital courses fall under the policies of publication of textbooks, art work, journal articles, and other endeavors traditionally undertaken by faculty? Or do digital courses fall under the "work for hire" arrangements often found outside of academia?

Though recent court cases have provided some guidance in this argument, as with all cases of law the guidance is individual to the elements of the decision. It seems that decisions are based on the institutional resources used, and on the nature of the job description associated with a specific individual or staff member. In general, it appears that:

- If the institution provides numerous resources to create the course (e.g. programmers, photographers, HTML coders, and hardware/software tools) outside of the input of the instructor, there may be a case for "work for hire."
- If the individual's job description specifically states he or she was hired to create online courses then there may be a foundation for the institution to claim a "work for hire" situation.
- On the other hand, if an individual was hired to teach a variety of courses, of which that individual may choose to deliver one in the online environment, there may not be a "work for hire" foundation.

Of course, the above scenarios are suppositions only, since the individual circumstances of each case would have a tremendous bearing on the outcome. Therefore, it benefits your institution to wrestle with these issues and devise a specific online intellectual property policy in advance and then to ensure that the policy is understood and accepted by faculty.

One well respected intellectual property policy model for online education was developed by the Stevens Institute of Technology in New Jersey. The policy primarily follows a traditional "publisher" model. It gives many of the rights and rewards for courses to the faculty members who develop them. Under the policy, faculty members are paid to develop online courses, will own the material in the courses they develop, and will control how and when that material can be used. The institution will control the copyrights of the online courses and will manage the courses' distribution. In return for giving up the copyright on a course, a faculty member receives a third of the revenue whenever a business or other institution purchases use of the course.

Faculty members who leave Stevens can take their courses to a new institution if it pays Stevens a licensing fee – in which case the professor would get a third of the money. This policy was overwhelmingly approved by the faculty and has been promulgated as a model to other institutions.

Several other institutions have created policies that simply give all copyright to the faculty member. These institutions believe that the amount of possible revenue in the sales of such courses is minimal compared with the costs to enforce copyright protections over the long term. In these institutions the faculty are allowed to receive any monies arising from the sale of their course based on the faculty member doing all the marketing and management of the sales process themselves. Usually, under these types of policies, the only negotiable item is that the educational institution will retain the right to continue using the course, without cost, even if the faculty member moves elsewhere.

Fortunately, it appears that the majority of educational institutions are promulgating the belief that non-restriction of course material is the best way to increase quality and knowledge in online learning. The example of the Massachusetts Institute of Technology in making available to the Web thousands of files containing professor notes and course activities exemplifies the belief in sharing resources. The encouragement of faculty and educational organizations to share course information, best practices, and implementation will ultimately benefit all educators and students. Furthermore, the more institutions and faculty are willing to share their work, the greater the savings in development and implementation costs.

For more information about intellectual property laws and practices around the world, an excellent Web resource is provided by Phillips Ormonde & Fitzpatrick at http://www.ipmenu.com/. Also, the Intellectual Property Law Server at http://www.intelproplaw.com/ provides several case law examples.

Changing technology: how to keep up

Over the past two decades, the pervasiveness and the nature of information technology resources in educational institutions have changed dramatically. Many educators have participated in the changing use of technology as institutions deployed mainframe batch-style computing, transitioned to timeshared services, adjusted to the dizzying proliferation of personal computers, and stretched to manage the networked computing environment.

It seems only yesterday that only a few selected instructors had computers in their office. In the early 1970s many institutions still required users to carry a stack of keypunched cards to the central computer center and return hours later to pick up the printout from the output bins. All the experts were also housed at the computer center, and users went there to seek their counsel when a program wouldn't work. Now we are each faced with mastering the computer on our desk. As personal computing has become mainstream, the expectation of individual knowledge of computing has grown; but the ability of individual faculty and administrators, as well as institutional experts, to keep up with technology has become difficult.

Personal considerations in keeping up with technology

Keeping up with technology is an issue both at an organizational and support level, as well as at a personal level. At a personal level, any educator involved with Web-based teaching and learning is faced with a plethora of resources (both on the Web and in print). The task of keeping current or even beginning to process all these resources is daunting. If you attempt to keep tabs on all the available resources – the Web, magazines, books, television shows, seminars, and so many others – you won't have time to do anything else . . . including your work. Below are some basic ideas for finding, sifting, and evaluating new technology resources on a personal level.

Information in print

Devote some time to perusing the technology magazine racks and reading educational journals that relate to technology. Journals and magazines exist that target all user levels. Try to find one or two that offer the kind of information you need, and which are written in a style you enjoy. Below is a listing of a few computer-related magazines that serve a general audience regarding hardware and software issues.

- *Windows Magazine*. This periodical covers much more than just Windows, although its primary focus is on operating systems and software issues. *Windows Magazine* provides the latest news on developments in operating systems, as well as tips for getting the best performance from your Windows PC. You can find reviews of applications and utilities, as well as information on hardware. Visit the *Windows Magazine* Web site at http://www.winmag.com/.
- *MacWorld*. This is one of the few magazines devoted exclusively to Macintosh computer users. *MacWorld* has a strong focus on graphics and desktop publishing issues, but pays plenty of attention to the world of Macintosh software and the Mac operating system. Hardware reviews abound, and the magazine provides tips for getting the most from your Mac. Visit the *MacWorld* Web site at http://www.macworld.com/.
- *Computer Shopper* focuses primarily on hardware, and on helping readers get the best deals on computer and communications equipment. There are lots of reviews, information about upgrading systems of all types, and (of course) advertisements. *Computer Shopper* may be one of the most ad-heavy magazines out there, but if you are interested in hardware, finding a good deal, or building your own PC, it's a good resource. Visit the *Computer Shopper* Web site at http://www.zdnet.com/computershopper/.
- *Byte* has long been considered a magazine for the advanced computer user, such as information systems managers, programmers, and database administrators. If you want a peek into higher-level technology issues, it is a good place to go. Like most tech magazines, *Byte* also offers product reviews and a great deal of opinion. Visit the *Byte* Web site at http://byte.com/.
- *Wired* magazine appeared not long after the World Wide Web came into prominence, and is required reading among "hip" computer users. *Wired* focuses on cutting-edge technologies, especially those that tie into the Internet or just seem cool. One unique aspect of *Wired* is its emphasis on the sociological issues surrounding technology. The editors do a great deal of prognosticating, some of which is daring, and much of which is humorously off the mark. *Wired* is famous for giving readers an insider's view of high-tech companies. Visit the *Wired* Web site at http://www.wired.com/.

In addition to the general computing magazines listed above, there are numerous journals for those interested in researching Web-based teaching and learning practices and experiences. A listing of some of the well respected, peer reviewed, print-based journals is below. Where Web links for information are available, they have been indicated.

- *American Journal of Distance Education* http://www.ed.psu.edu/acsde/ Jour.html
- *Distance Education: An International Journal* http://www.usq.edu.au/dec/ decjourn/demain.htm
- *Educational Technology Research and Development* (*ETR&D*)
- *EDUCAUSE Quarterly* http://www.educause.edu/pub/eq/eq.html
- *International Journal of Continuing Engineering Education and Life-long Learning* (*IJCEELLL*) http://www.mscp.edte.utwente.nl/ptk/
- *International Journal of Educational Technology* http://www.outreach.uius. edu/ijet/
- *International Journal of Educational Telecommunications* http://www.aace.org/ pubs/ijet/default.htm
- *Journal of Educational Multimedia and Hypermedia* (*JEMH*) http://www.aace. org/pubs/jemh/default.htm
- *Journal of Interactive Learning Research* (*JILR*) http://www.aace.org/ pubs/jilr/
- *Journal of Technology and Teacher Education* (*JTATE*) http://www.aace.org/ pubs/jtate/default.htm

There are a number of Web sites that provide an annotated bibliography of journals, newsletters, and magazines in the field along with links to associated pages. Three of these sites are:

- http://Webster.commnet.edu/HP/pages/darling/journals.htm
- http://olt-bta.hrdc-drhc.gc.ca/info/eljoue.html
- http://ericir.syr.edu/ithome/edutech.htm

Online resources

Magazines and journals are a good way to get news and information, but they also have drawbacks. First, they can be expensive. Second, if you don't take time to read them, they go to waste. Third, they pile up fast. For those reasons and others, you may prefer to get a daily dose of technology news delivered to your desktop via the Internet. Of course, there are many times more Web sites than magazines, but if you are selective, you can get just the amount and type of information you need. Here are some tips for keeping up with technology through online resources.

- *Create a personalized start page.* Using a "portal" Web site, such as Microsoft Network (http://www.msn.com/), Yahoo! (http://www.yahoo.com/), Snap (http://www.snap.com/), and others, you can set up a custom start page that opens each time you launch your browser. Portal sites allow you to add features to your start page, such as updated weather, movie listings, and news. Depending on the portal you use, you may be able to select a "computer" or "technology" option that delivers tech-related news headlines to your desktop. Some sites allow you to set parameters for your news, as well. For example, you may be able to set your start page to display up-to-the-minute news reports about specific subjects, such as e-learning, wireless communications, or technology debates in higher education.

- *Use a good search engine*. Nearly all search engines post categorized news stories on their home pages and update them several times each day. Simply visit your favorite search engine and check the headlines. For news related specifically to computers and technology, click the "Computers" or "Computers and Internet" link. If you want to search the Web for other articles, start your search from the "Computers" page; that will narrow your search results by focusing on computer-related indexes. Many users set up a search engine as their start page; many search engines now offer all the features of a portal site, enabling you to customize your start page and access advanced search tools the instant you launch your browser.

- *Find a good online dictionary*. If you come across a new computer-related term, you can probably find a definition on the Internet. Popular Web-based technology dictionaries include PC Webopedia (http://www.pcWebopedia.com/), the Digital Diva (http://www.microsoft.com/digitaldiva/), and SmartComputing (http:www.smartcomputing.com/).

- *Subscribe to a newsletter*. Most of the online magazines (listed in the preceding section) offer free online newsletters. To register for a free newsletter, visit the magazine's Web site and click the link that lets you subscribe. You will need to provide your e-mail address. Some sites let you customize your newsletter by specifying your particular interests. Be careful not to subscribe to too many newsletters, however, or you will find yourself inundated with information. Also, be sure to read the site's privacy policies and make sure your e-mail address won't be given out or sold to marketers; otherwise you may receive a lot of junk mail.

- *Subscribe to a list-serve* specific to online education issues. DEOS-L is such a list-serve provided by Pennsylvania State University. DEOS-L has been (and continues to be) a very active moderated list-serve for over ten years. It facilitates discussion of current issues in distance education and serves over 5,000 subscribers in eighty countries. Discussions on DEOS-L include: current controversies, new speculations, and topical issues; research inquiries and requests for assistance; professional networking; announcements of conferences and job opportunities. You can join the list at: http://lists.psu.edu/cgi-bin/wa?SUBED1=deos-l&A=1.

- *Join a newsgroup*. There are hundreds of Internet newsgroups devoted to computing and technology issues. To find them, launch your newsreader and search for newsgroups with "comp" in their name (such as comp.edu or comp.lang.javascript). In a newsgroup, you can join a discussion about a specific topic or simply read other people's postings. Be aware, however, that some newsgroups are notorious sources of rumors and misinformation. Watch a newsgroup for a while before deciding whether it is a credible source of information. Better yet, look for newsgroups that are moderated.

- *Online journals.* There are a number of online journals that also relate to Web-based education issues. A listing of some of the popular sites is below.
  Asynchronous Learning Networks (ALN), http://www.aln.org/
  Canadian Journal of Distance Education (CADE), http://cade.icaap.org/
  European Journal of Open and Distance Learning Interactions, http://www.nks.no/eurodl
  International Review of Research in Open and Distance Learning (IRRODL), http://www.irrodl.org
  Journal of Distance Learning Administration, http://www.westga.edu/~distance/jmain11.html
  Online Chronicle of Distance Education and Communication, http://www.fcae.nova.edu/disted/index.html
  The Technology Source, http://horizon.unc.edu/

It's easy to become overwhelmed by all the information you find. Here are some guidelines that can help you avoid infoglut (a term that refers to a flood of information, a large percentage of which may be irrelevant to your needs) while getting all the technology information you want:

- *Define your interests.* If you are new to computers, your interests may be general. If you have been around computers for a while, you may want to focus on specific aspects of technology, such as creating MOOS and MUDs for simulation exercises in education. Because so much information is available on so many topics, it pays to target your interests and focus on them.
- *Be selective about the materials you choose to read.* Regardless of your interests or level of expertise, you can easily find dozens of information sources that seem relevant to your needs. To avoid getting overwhelmed, review your resources carefully. Decide which ones best meet your needs and are most enjoyable. At first, limit yourself to one or two information sources; add new ones as your needs or reading habits change.
- *Limit the amount of time you spend keeping up to date.* Keeping up to date on technology is a lifelong pursuit, but it shouldn't take up all your time. Set aside an amount of time each day for reviewing the latest technology news, just as you devote thirty minutes a day to watching the evening news. Limiting your time can help you stay focused on the issues that are important to you.
- *Leverage online resources.* You can subscribe to magazines that interest you, but you may want to consider using the Internet as your primary source of technology news. Why? First, the majority of Web sites and online magazines are free. Second, the best ones are updated daily – not weekly or monthly. Third, most offer search tools to help you find exactly the kind of information

you want. Fourth, some provide e-mail updates that notify you when articles matching your interests are posted.

A final word of advice may be the most important: don't become a slave to information. Convinced that knowledge is power, the classic "infoglut victim" feels he or she must absorb every shred of information that makes its way to the desktop. This is a misconception. *All* knowledge is not power, but the *right* knowledge is a powerful thing indeed. Don't waste time reading every e-mail message, article, report, and advertisement you see. Master the art of skimming. Decide which information is most interesting or useful to you, then get rid of the rest. You won't miss reading the articles you don't need.

Institutional considerations in distributed computing and keeping up with technology

Beyond the individual difficulties of keeping up with technology lie the bigger issues of institutional difficulties. Today the distribution of computing responsibility has become a part of many job descriptions in education. In some institutions every department has system managers, and the computing systems they are individually managing are more powerful and complex than the one encased in glass with its own mysterious experts in years past. Educational institutions today operate at least 10,000 times the amount of computational capacity of the early 1970s. The problem has been that many institutions are still behaving as if they are still managing that single computer. Others have realized that things have changed, but are behaving as though the distributed desktops are independent, self-contained environments like they were when the "personal" in "personal computer" meant just that. Today's networked machines can no longer be treated as simply personal.

As the bulk of computing has moved to desktops that are linked to the rest of the world through powerful networks, the need for support has developed outside of the computer center as well as within. It is both ineffective and inefficient to provide only centralized support in a distributed technology environment. It is ineffective because central staff cannot understand the diverse needs and abilities of users as fully as support staff who focus on specific subsets of users. It is inefficient because many problems are relatively easy to resolve if the helper is at the user's desktop, but much more difficult when the helper is physically unable to experience the desktop directly.

As organizations grow, the processes of communication and coordination consume more and more resources, subtracting from those available for directly productive work. Very large universities and school districts, in particular, might profit from smaller units of support.

Technology systems are very complex. No single person or group can fully understand either the technology or the range of applications desired by diverse users. Complete self-support by each user now is out of the question. Where groups of relatively similar applications and needs are clustered, as in academic departments, targeted support staff are more likely to provide high-quality support. This is especially true if they concentrate on the departments' unique areas and if they have good access to central staff who concentrate on common needs and basic infrastructure.

Linking to central staff is equally important to providing departmental support. If the people who provide support do not also function in a linked relationship, it will be increasingly difficult to provide effective services on a system-wide basis. This point is clear when you consider the interconnectedness of a simple use, such as looking up an entry in the library catalog. In this case, the desktop is probably managed by the user or, at best, the user's department; the local area network is usually managed by the department; the wide area network is managed by the telecommunications department; and the internet connection may be provided by an external state or regional network. The local servers might be managed by what used to be the "computer center", or perhaps the library, and the application might be managed by the local library or, sometimes, by a remote state consortium of libraries. Each of these technical links is managed by different people with different work priorities and cultures. As complex as getting the technology to work, getting the human support network to function is of even more importance and frequently much more difficult.

Hardware and software costs are generally only a quarter to a third of the total costs of distributed computing environments. It is the costs of technical support, training, and management of the desktop environment that have created the high cost of distributed computing in most institutions. One way to lower costs is to manage the standard parts of a standard desktop environment in a standard way, centrally, through the network, while focusing distributed support staff on unique applications and needs. This requires defining and enforcing standard computer configurations, standard software allowed on those computers, and standard user training.

It seems that higher education institutions have tended to evolve a haphazard model of support based on individual faculty and individual departments selecting products, hardware, and software that meet their specific needs. This results in one department using Macintosh machines while another uses PCs. One department uses Microsoft's suite of products while another uses Lotus. In some institutions this also applies to Web-based course development. One professor will use WebCT, another uses Blackboard, an entire department contracts with E-college for online courses, and yet another encourages individual Web pages and Javascript coding for its courses.

This reluctance toward standardization is couched in terms of protest about "academic freedom" and "meeting the needs of students." However, more often the selection of tools lies in the comfort level of a few individuals who happened to have learned a particular tool early in their computing adoption process and are now unwilling to learn another. This haphazard model of support creates very high costs for little benefit. People find ways to get the support they need by creating new technology-related positions in each department and by refusing to coordinate with other institutional support structures for fear they will need to change. In this environment, costs continue to rise, support is inconsistent and inefficient, and staff will naturally take independent and inconsistent positions on important technical and support issues.

These institutional discontinuities will result in a wide variety of problems ranging well beyond first-level waste. E-mail attachments may not be easily shared across the institution; faculty and students whose work crosses the borders between service domains may receive inconsistent and conflicting technical advice; mistakes on such fundamental levels as cabling types may occur. Once a haphazard model has become well established, it can be difficult to replace because of intense vested interests in the *status quo*, even if the *status quo* is acknowledged as being inadequate.

The ultimate goal, of course, is to help institutions provide the best possible opportunities for learning, research, and outreach. Effective technology support can contribute directly to achieving these goals by enabling faculty, staff, and students to funnel their time and energy directly and effectively into learning activities and institutional support processes rather than wasting resources struggling with computers, applications, and networks. McClure *et al.* (2000) outline several strategies to help achieve this goal:

- Couple institutional infrastructure and standards to the real needs and priorities of end users.
- Provide a reliable and robust infrastructure that provides users with a guaranteed level of functionality.
- Establish a mechanism for communication among users, local support staff, and central staff.
- Enhance technical skill levels of local and central staff and users through a consistent training program in standards, while providing an additional focus on unique and discipline-specific user needs for distributed support personnel.

If a haphazard model is not effective, what type of model is best? There exists no one "best" model for distributed support. Below are four models that may work for this type of infrastructure. It is also possible that an institution would best be served by combining models to meet their specific needs.

Administrative unit model

This is the most common model. Each organizational unit, usually defined by budget responsibility at some level, has one or more support staff managed on behalf of members of the unit. Sometimes the unit is large, for example, a school, and the sizable staff make up an organized group that specializes in certain functions, applications, or technologies. In other instances the unit is a small department, and a single generalist comprises the support group.

Discipline model

Another effective model groups departments into clusters based on disciplinary similarity. Examples are clusters in foreign languages, humanities, physical sciences, biomedical sciences, social sciences, and fine arts. Discipline-based organizations are probably less common because many institutions' budgets do not correspond to these groupings, which makes it difficult for units to cooperate and share resources across departments. The model has much to recommend it, however, if departmental politics and budget structures can accommodate it. The most obvious benefit is that better support can be provided for very small units which, on their own, may not be in a position to dedicate even a single person to technology support.

Less obvious, but perhaps more important, is that such an organization makes it more likely that common problems and issues can be addressed efficiently. Foreign-language word processing is an example. The effort required for each language department to identify, implement, and develop expertise in such functionality would be much greater than if they worked on the general problem together. Another advantage is that technology support resources often serve as a vehicle for collaboration among faculty across disciplines.

Precincts model

In this model, the physical campus is divided into contiguous units. Technology staff are assigned to support those housed in buildings in close proximity. This model works well when the support staff are primarily focused at the infrastructure rather than the application level, or on common standard applications, and/or if the units in a discipline are widely dispersed across the campus. It serves to minimize the transit time of support staff and keep them available at or near a base of operations. It can also help bond staff to their customers and create a greater service orientation. Because many campuses are laid out such that disciplines are clustered physically into precincts, the discipline and precinct models are often the same.

Functional model

In this model, specialized support groups are organized to serve different institutional functions. For example, individual support groups might include research computing, instructional technology, and administrative processes. These may or may not report to and be co-located with the central technology support staff. The research group may report to the vice-president for research; the instructional technology group may report to the provost; the administrative processes group may report to the chief financial officer. The advantage of this scheme is its focus on core activities that are identifiable by faculty and staff. It can lead to greater depth of expertise, but it also can run into trouble if responsibilities for all common hardware and software support are not clearly delegated elsewhere. A single faculty member is at the same time a researcher, a teacher, and sometimes an administrator. All aspects of that person's work should occur in a coherent environment.

Matching technology communication mechanisms is key

Communication is key to keeping up with technology today. In the distributed support model, the amount of information is vast, some of it is very esoteric, and most of it is irrelevant to a particular user or support provider. The eternal communications paradox is that if you provide all the information, most of it will be ignored, including the relevant parts. The only realistic solution is to provide all of the information in as many formats as possible, and to provide selection and filtering mechanisms to route the correct information to the people who need it, when they need it. Local support providers are most knowledgeable about the use and needs of their departments. These local support personnel can become the bi-directional filter. They pass on to their people only the technical information that is relevant to the users' needs.

Because no single communications mechanism will serve all the users, it is important to use every possible mode, from personal contact to articles in the campus newspaper. With clever planning and design, information can be organized to fit into multiple formats with minimal extra effort, e.g. the announcement of a change in service can be placed in the campus technology newsletter, the campus newspaper, on bulletin boards, in a list-serve message, on the technology announcements Web page, and in the distributed support providers' newsgroup. It is still necessary, however, to place some priorities on messages. Although everything is important to someone, not everything is important to everyone.

Matching the communications mechanism used with the mechanism favored by the individual is essential. Some people prefer "impersonal" electronic messages. Others need human contact in order to best receive the message. Some people look forward to weekly or monthly meetings, while others go to great lengths to avoid them. It is easy, particularly when dealing with limited resources, to say, "We made it available, it's your fault if you didn't take advantage of it." Communication is so vital in distributed support that every reasonable effort must be made to make the information easily available, in the style best received by those who need it.

It is essential to establish communication mechanisms that let users control when, as well as how, they get the information they need. For example, users don't need to understand mail-merge in detail until they need to send out 100 letters. Even if they were given that information in an introductory course, they are likely to have forgotten it by the time they need it. Short and simple messages can announce new information, with greater detail available via electronic or human linking. Indexing and cataloging of information are important tools in helping both users and providers find the information they need, at the most appropriate level of detail.

Accreditation of online degree programs

There has been some concern voiced over the efficacy of online degree programs versus traditional residential programs. These accreditation issues have become particularly important in the case of commercial institutions of higher education that are now totally virtual – they have no residential campus base at all.

In the United States, accreditation of higher education rests in six regional authorities. It is the responsibility of these authorities to ensure that the quality of education required to attain specific degree levels is somewhat consistent across the nation. Some argue that while online courses from traditional institutions may have the ability to show some equivalence of standards, totally online institutions raise questions about the meaning and preservation of higher education itself. Some of the key issues raised by protesters of such accreditation are:

- With classrooms, libraries, and faculty members located somewhere in cyberspace, how can the university be evaluated effectively?
- Can we really call those institutions "colleges" or "universities" if they lack both a critical core of full-time faculty members and a system of governance by which the faculty is responsible for developing curricula and academic policy?
- How can accreditors actually determine that new online institutions meet the same basic criteria for quality – or, at least, equivalent criteria – that traditional accredited institutions must meet?
- Does accreditation of institutions that do not require or support research undermine the standard of research that nourishes and informs teaching and learning?

The fear is that courses prepared by a "content expert" and an instructional designer, then delivered by a "faculty facilitator" in a uniform manner, turns education into modular units that disrupt or preclude the critical interaction between students and faculty members.

These are significant questions and ones that should certainly be considered by any institution, whether wholly virtual or not, when evaluating the quality of the education. However, it is also important not to become hidebound by a tradition that is based in brick-and-mortar walls. The key is to assume that quality must be present for accreditation, not that quality is lost in the virtual world.

In answer to the naysayers, the accrediting bodies have provided several guidelines for accreditation of online curricula for any institution. These are as follows:

- An online curriculum, like that of any traditional college or university, must have a clearly articulated educational mission, state-government approval to operate and grant degrees, and a governing board with a strong contingent of representatives of the public.
- It must provide accurate information to students about its programs and must demonstrate fiscal stability, which includes providing externally audited financial statements.
- It must offer its students access to resources and services, such as libraries, that are needed for its degree programs.
- All institutions must prepare a detailed self-study document, containing evidence to support the claim that they meet the standards of accreditation. Then,

to determine the accuracy of the self-study, experienced teams of peer reviewers – including experts in distance and adult education, extended library services, and finance, as well as specialists in the specific curricula up for accreditation – make several site visits to the corporate offices and educational headquarters. The teams also interview students, staff, and administrators by phone and e-mail to determine the accuracy of the self-study.

Additionally, virtual courses are evaluated on specific technology-related guidelines such as those set out below:

- Does the institution use technology that is appropriate to the objectives of the program?
- Does it offer faculty support services specifically related to distance education?
- Does it provide help to students who are experiencing difficulty in using the required technology?
- Have appropriately degreed and accredited, knowledgeable people in each field of study defined the content and presentation of the curriculum?
- Do the students' learning experiences allow effective interaction, both between faculty members and students and among students?
- Is there a valid system for evaluating student achievement?

In short, it appears that the accreditation of online programs or wholly virtual universities in the United States follows the same standards as those for accrediting traditional campus-based universities. Will the fears of some academics become realized in the future or will the new wave of virtual courses eventually be accepted, and perhaps become models of educational delivery? The outcome is unknown, but it is certain that the virtual university will not disappear in the near future. In fact, there is a larger movement both nationally and abroad for certification of specific student knowledge and skills rather than accreditation of entire colleges and universities.

Certification has already become the standard in technical fields such as computer science and engineering. Employers in these fields are often more concerned about specific certifications than about academic degrees. It is hard to know whether this trend toward certification is good or bad. But it certainly speaks to an unmet need in the field. Perhaps there is a way to work together to provide the certification needed and still infuse the characteristic qualities of critical thinking, analysis, and synthesis that are associated with higher education and are often left unmeasured in specific certifications.

Future trends

With the onward march of technology and the rich investment of money, as well as the development of hundreds of content products on the market for Web-based education, there is no doubt that the virtual classroom is just beginning to approach the arduous, steep climb toward its peak marketability. The online education market is predicted to be the largest sector of technology-based education by 2002, with a dollar growth to over $1 billion in the United States alone. Products will continue to develop for the production and distribution of educational content. The question is whether campuses will use those products in a continued attempt to transfer the entrenched traditional models of teaching and learning in the campus-based classroom or whether some new, innovative models specific to Web-based delivery will be developed and become successful.

Course development products continue to grow

It is likely that products will continue to develop the following features.

- Course management and tracking tools
- Easier Web page-building tools
- Online testing and feedback tools
- Increased search and bookmarking tools
- Improved user single authentication environments

With growing investment in Internet bandwidth, it is also probable that in the first decade of the new century tools for audio, video, and other real-time communication will be enhanced and used more frequently. Some industry experts are predicting inexpensive bandwidth increases that will be available worldwide. In the interim, the use of mobile agents – such as efficiency and network traffic reduction, synchronous autonomous interaction, local processing of data, interaction with real-time entities – will address connection unreliability and bandwidth limitations.

Internet availability and access will expand

Many countries around the world are funding large-scale projects to enhance accessibility. For example, the European Commission has developed its eEurope Action Plan. The following key elements are expected to be in place by 2002:

- The Internet will become a part of every child's education.
- Lower Internet access costs and a faster service will become a reality.
- Students and researchers will be enabled to work and learn collaboratively over the Internet.
- Secure access to services will be provided using multifunctional smart cards.
- Access to government services will be provided in 'Internet time'.

For more information see the EC Web site at http://europa.eu.int/rapid/start/cgi/guesten.ksh?p_action.gettxt=gt&doc=IP/00/514|0|RAPID&lg=EN. Other countries such as India, China, and Russia also have made significant investments in creating better Internet access.

Movements toward standardization will grow

The movement toward standardization of datasets and thus easier sharing of content and activity objects will increase. Already two key standards groups have had their first versions accepted by international representatives from many educational institutions.

- *IMS* The International Meta-data Specification consortium has been working since the 1990s on open specifications for the technical building blocks of online learning. They have worked with thousands of educational institutions around the world to create a comprehensive approach and focus on infrastructure. In 2000 the technical board unanimously approved Version 1.0 of the IMS Content Packaging Specification and the IMS Question and Test Interoperability Specification, as well as Version 1.1 of the IMS Learning Resources Meta-data Specification. For more information on these important standards see http://www.imsproject.org.
- *SCORM* is a set of specifications and guidelines that facilitate the development of interoperable, reusable, and accessible content. This allows easier moving of learning content from one management system to another (e.g. from WebCT to Blackboard or to a proprietary system using SCORM) or to reuse or integrate content. After considerable vetting and verification, SCORM Version 1.1 was released in 2001. Proponents state that studies have shown that the use of interoperable objects reduces the costs of instruction development and delivery by 30–60 percent. Already several course tool vendors have adopted the specifications.

Organizations will continue to join together to share resources

The cost of technology and the need for experts in developing curriculum that works with virtual classrooms has generated several educational consortiums for the virtual school environment. England has been a leader in this effort, with its Open University environment that encourages people of all educational levels to engage in continuing learning opportunities. This open learning concept has spread to other countries as well.

In the United States, many schools (both public and private) have begun to recognize the wealth of opportunity to be gained in joining together. Some have formed electronic colleges at a state level, made up of classes generated by many member state schools. Some private institutions have gone a step further and physically merged campus administrations in order to capitalize on curriculum needs (e.g. one campus brings a law school to the table while another brings a medical school). Yet others have formed interstate or even international consortiums to meet the needs of students across many borders. On the K-12 level a similar, though smaller, sharing of resources is also occurring. Multiple districts sometimes join together. State governments are appointing technology liaisons to the schools and encouraging shared Web-based resources.

All of this combining and sharing has begun to create an atmosphere that promotes working toward meeting student needs and developing individual specialties that can be combined across borders, and decreasing the competitive nature born of fighting for student registrations. That is not to say that competition has died or that it will disappear. However, the possibility of a new paradigm for educational delivery that encourages shared resources and yet promises ongoing prosperity is slowly emerging.

Embracing change

We are at a critical juncture in the virtual education growth curve. The pace of change in digital technology, coupled with worldwide communication capabilities, has provided us with a unique opportunity to make profound changes in teaching and learning. We need only to find the courage to embrace change and mold it to enhance the teaching and learning environment.

Already, publishers are providing individualized digital content for textbooks. Professors or departments can mix and match pages and chapters from several books or magazines held by the publisher to create specific content needed for their classes. Libraries are investing heavily in digital collections of books, journals, and art works for delivery over the Web. Personal portal development has come into its own, allowing users to design the content they want to immediately access. Using XML (eXtensible Markup Language) Microsoft plans to develop a common platform for different computer languages and end-user devices, freeing programmers to focus on strategy and reusing code instead of constantly learning new languages.

Finally, the ubiquitous availability of communication tools such as video and audio (and others we cannot even yet imagine) may well make the physical separation of learners and teachers moot. Our ability to use these tools to provide a rich and extensive one-to-one, student-specific learning environment will be the test of our desire to embrace and use these changes – to adopt an ideal of sharing resources, control, and power in education in order to provide our students with the knowledge and skills they will need in our increasingly technical and complex world.

There are many visions of the future of virtual classrooms. However, one that is particularly poignant and seems to comfortably embrace the changes of technology and education discussed above was posted on the DEOS list-serve by John Hibbs in 2001. It is used here with his permission and seems a fitting ending for this book – an ending filled with hope for the future of education.

In my academic picture each university will have areas of truly world class strength, of a kind so attractive that its courses would be exportable and in large demand. These universities would have a culture as vigorous in their quest to import excellence as it is to export their focused undertakings. It is a 'picture' of rich diversity where the bonds to the residential campus remain forever cemented; a place where students in Idaho majoring in forestry would be encouraged to take Spanish literature from Madrid, with classmates from China and Australia and West Africa. In my university of the future, the benefits from the virtual world would help to enhance that of the physical.

(John Hibbs, Benjamin Franklin University)

References

American Association for Higher Education (2000) *Nine Principles of Good Practice for Assessing Student Learning*, available online at http://www.aahe.org/assessment/principl.htm

Angelo, T. (1999) "Doing assessment as if learning matters most," *AAHE Bulletin*, available online at http://www.aah.org/Bulletin/angelomay99.htm

Australian Bureau of Statistics Database, *Computer Users and Internet Users in 1998*, report available at http://www.abs.gov.AU/

Bates, A. (1988) "Television, learning, and distance education," *Journal of Education Television* **14** (3), 213–25.

—— (1991) "Third generation distance education: the challenge of new technology," *Research in Distance Education* **3** (2), 109–15.

Bereiter, C., and Scardamalia, M. (2000) "Beyond Bloom's taxonomy: rethinking knowledge for the knowledge age," Ontario Institute for Studies in Education, University of Toronto. Available online at http://www.csile.oisc.utoronto.ca/abstracts/Piaget.html

Bloom, B. S., ed. (1956) *Taxonomy of Educational Objectives: the Classification of Educational Goals*. Handbook I, *Cognitive Domain*, New York: Longman.

Bonk, C., and Reynolds, T. (1997) "Learner-centered Web instruction for higher-order thinking, teamwork, and apprenticeship," in Badrul Khan (ed.) *Web-based Instruction*, Englewood Cliffs NJ: Educational Technology Publications.

Bonk, C., Reynolds, T., and Medury, P. (1996) "Technology enhanced workplace writing: a social and cognitive transformation," in A. H. Dunn and C. J. Hansen (eds) *Non-academic Writing: Social Theory and Technology*, Mahwah NJ: Erlbaum.

Browser Watch Stats Station (2001) available online at http://browserwatch.internet.com/stats.html

Campbell, R. (1998) "Hyperminds for hypertimes: the demise of rational, logical thought?", *Educational Technology* **38** (1), 24–31.

Carley, K., and Palmquist, M. (1992) "Extracting, representing, and analyzing mental models," *Social Forces* **70** (3), 601–36.

CIA World Factbook (2000), accessed for population statistics; available online at http://www.odci.gov/cia/publications/factbook/index.html

Collis, B. A., Parisi, D., and Ligono, B. (1996) "Adaptation of courses for trans-European tele-learning," *Journal of Computer-assisted Learning* **12** (1), 47–62.

Computer Industry Almanac (2000) estimate of Internet users in fifty countries from 1990 to 2000, with projections for each year, 2001–05, Arlington Heights IL: Computer Industry Almanac.

Cornell, R., and Martin, B. (1997) "The role of motivation in web-based instruction," in Badrul Khan (ed.) *Web-based Instruction*, Englewood Cliffs NJ: Educational Technology Publications.

Dille, B., and Mezack, M. (1991) "Identifying predictors of high risk among community college telecourse students," *American Journal of Distance Education* **5** (1), 24–35.

Donlan, L. (1998) "Visions of online projects dance in my head," *Multimedia Schools* **5** (1), 20–2.

Eanes, R. (2001) "Task-oriented question construction wheel based on Bloom's taxonomy," St Edward's University Center of Excellence, available online at http://www.stedwards.edu/cte/bwheel.htm

Edge, S., and Edge, D. (1998) "Building library support for distance learning through collaboration," *Libraries without Walls* II, *The Delivery of Library Services to Distance Users*, London: Library Association, http://www.la-q.org.uk/directory/publications.html

English, F. (1978) *Quality Control in Curriculum Development*, Arlington VA: American Association of School Administrators.

Entwistle, N., and Ramsden, P. (1983) *Understanding Student Learning*, London: Croom Helm.

Hara, N., and Kling, R. (2000) "Students' Distress with a Web-based Distance Education Course," CSI Working Paper, available June 1, 2000, online at http://www.slis.indiana.edu/CSI/wp00-01.html.

Harasim, L. (1997) "Interacting in hyperspace," in University of Maryland System Institute for Distance Education and International University Consortium Conference on Learning, *Teaching Interacting in Hyperspace: The Potential of the Web*. Available 10 October 1998 online at: http://www2.ncsu.edu/ncsu/cc/pub/teachtools/ConfReport.htm

Harasim, L., Hiltz, S., Teles, L., and Turoff, M. (1997) *Learning Networks: A Field Guide to Teaching and Learning Online*, Cambridge MA: MIT Press.

Heldref Publications (1999) "Gauging the impact of institutional student-assessment strategies," *Change* **31** (5), 53–7.

Henschke, J. A. (1998) "Modeling the preparation of adult educators," *Adult Learning* **9** (3), 11–13.

Hiltz, S. (1994) *The Virtual Classroom: Learning without Limits via Computer Networks*, Norwood NJ: Ablex.

Holloway, R. E., and Ohler, J. (1991) "Distance education in the next decade," in G. J. Anglin (ed.) *Instructional Technology, Past, Present, and Future*, Englewood Cliffs NJ: Libraries Unlimited.

Imel, S. (1994) *Guidelines for Working with Adult Learners*, ERIC Digest No. 154, accession No. ED377313, Columbus OH: ERIC Clearing House on Adult, Career, and Vocational Education.

IT News at NineMSN. "E-learning Firms cram for European Test," report available online at http://news.ninemsn.com.au/itnews/story_7915.asp

Jonassen, D. (1995) "Operationalizing Mental Models: Strategies for assessing Mental Models to support Meaningful Learning and Design-supportive Learning Environments," available online at http://www-csc195.indiana.edu/csc195/jonassen.html

Keller, J., and Burkman, E. (1993) "Motivation principles," in M. Fleming and W. H. Levie (eds) *Instructional Message Design: Principles from the Behavioral and Cognitive Sciences*, second edition, Englewood Cliffs NJ: Educational Technology Publications.

Kemp, J., Morrison, G., and Ross, S. (1998) *Designing Effective Instruction*, second edition, Upper Saddle River NJ: Prentice-Hall.

Kirk, E., and Bartelstein, A. (1999) "Libraries close in on distance education," *Library Journal* **124** (6), 40–2.

Knowles, M. (1984) *Andragogy in Action: Applying Modern Principles of Adult Education*, San Francisco: Jossey-Bass.

Kolb, D. (1986) *Learning Style Inventory: Technical Manual*, revised edition, Boston MA: McBer.

Kwan, K. (1999) "How fair are student ratings in assessing the teaching performance of university teachers?", *Assessment and Evaluation in Higher Education* **24** (2), 181–96.

McClure, P., Smith, J., and Lockard, T. (2000) *Distributed Computing*, Bloomington IN: Indiana University Press.

McVay, M. (1998) "Facilitating Knowledge Construction and Communication on the Internet," *Technology Source*, available online at http://horizon.unc.edu/TS/default. asp?show=article&id=60

—— (2000a) *How to be a Successful Distance Learning Student: Learning on the Internet*, second edition, Needham Heights MA: Pearson.

—— (2000b) "Developing a Web-based Distance Student Orientation to enhance Student Success in an Online Bachelor's Degree Completion Program," doctoral dissertation, North Miami Beach FL: Nova Southeastern University.

Moore, M. (1992) "Distance education theory," *American Journal of Distance Education* **5** (3), 1–6.

Moore, M., and Kearsley, G. (1996) *Distance Education: A Systems View*, Belmont CA: Wadsworth.

NEA Higher Education – Advocate Online (2001) "Course Web Sites: Are they Worth the Effort?", National Education Association, available at http://www.nea.org/he/advo-new/feature.html

Neill, Judy (1998) "Practice makes learning," in *Distance Learning '98: Proceedings of the* [fourteenth] *Annual Conference on Distance Teaching and Learning*, August 5–7, Madison WI: University of Wisconsin.

Nelson, T. H. (1973) "A conceptual framework for man – machine everything," *AFIPS Conference Proceedings*, Montvale NJ: American Federation of Information Processing Societies.

Pea, R. (1994) "Seeing what we build together: distributed multimedia learning environments for transformative communications," *Journal of the Learning Sciences* **3** (3), 285–99.

Ravitz, J. (1997) "Evaluating learning networks: a special challenge for Web-based instruction," in B. Khan (ed.) *Web-based Instruction*, Englewood Cliffs NJ: Educational Technology Publications.

Reigeluth, C. (1995) "The imperative for systemic change," in C. M. Reigeluth and R. Garfinkle (eds) *Systemic Change in Education*, Englewood Cliffs NJ: Educational Technology Publications.

Ridley, D., and Husband, J. (1998) "Online education: a study of academic rigor and integrity," *Journal of Instructional Psychology* **25** (3), 184–8.

Romiszowski, A. J. (1997) "Web-based distance learning and teaching: revolutionary invention or reaction to necessity?", in Badrul Khan (ed.) *Web-based Instruction*, Englewoods Cliffs NJ: Educational Technology Publications.

Sherry, L., and Wilson, B. (1997) "Transformative communication as a stimulus to Web innovations," in Badrul Khan (ed.) *Web-based Instruction*, Englewood Cliffs NJ: Educational Technology Publications.

Shotsberger, P. (1994) "Emerging roles for instructors and learners in the Web-based instruction classroom," in Barry Willis (ed.) *Distance Education: Strategies and Tools*, Englewood Cliffs NJ: Educational Technology Publications.

StatMarket, used for a variety of web statistics at http://www.statmarket.com

Terrell, S., and Dringus, L. (1999) "An investigation of the effect of learning style on student success in an online learning environment," *Journal of Educational Technology Systems* **28** (3), 231–8.

Torrance, E. (1972) "Teaching for creativity," *Journal of Creative Behavior* **6**, 114–43.

Williams, V., and Peters, K. (1994) "Faculty incentives for the preparation of Web-based instruction," in Barry Willis (ed.) *Distance Education: Strategies and Tools*, Englewood Cliffs NJ: Educational Technology Publications.

Willis, B. (1994) "Enhancing faculty effectiveness in distance education," in Barry Willis (ed.) *Distance Education: Strategies and Tools*, Englewood Cliffs NJ: Educational Technology Publications.

Willis, C. R. (1998) "Knowledge construction in teacher-development practices," *Educational Forum* **62** (4), 306–15.

Wilson, B., and Ryder, M. (1998) "Distributed Learning Communities: an Alternative to Designed Instructional Systems," available online at http://carbon.cudenver.edu/~bwilson/dlc.html

Yanni, M. (2000) 'Technology is us: do we have time to learn?", *Tech Trends* **44** (4), 42–3.

Index